Simon Parkin is an award winning critic and journalist. His articles exploring the vibrant culture that has grown up around video games have featured in the *New Yorker*, *New Scientist*, *New Statesman* and the *Guardian*.

Praise for *Death by Video Game*

'Parkin guides us with grace, intelligence and without judgment through the shades and the dark levels of our medium' Martin Hollis, director of *Goldeneye 007* and *Perfect Dark*

'Simon Parkin's surgical story-telling reveals the humanity, beauty and truth beneath the surface of our digital adventuring' Jonathan Smith, Director of the National Videogame Arcade

'*Death by Video Game* is *life* by video games. Simon Parkin is gaming's Jon Ronson, and his book charts the extremes of the medium to try to answer the question *why the hell do we all care about video games anyway?*' Kieron Gillen, writer of *Iron Man*, *Uncanny X-Men* and *The Wicked + The Divine*, co-founder of *Rock, Paper, Shotgun*

'The best book about video games I've read since I wrote one' Steven Poole, author of *Trigger Happy*

DEATH
BY VIDEO
GAME

TALES OF OBSESSION FROM THE VIRTUAL FRONTLINE

SIMON PARKIN

A complete catalogue record for this book can
be obtained from the British Library on request

The right of Simon Parkin to be identified as the author of this work has been
asserted by him in accordance with the Copyright, Designs and Patents Act 1988

First published in 2015 by Serpent's Tail,
an imprint of Profile Books Ltd
3 Holford Yard
Bevin Way
London WC1X 9HD
www.serpentstail.com

ISBN 978 1 78125 421 9
eISBN 978 1 78283 143 3

Designed and typeset by Crow Books

Printed and bound in Great Britain by Clays, St Ives plc

10 9 8 7 6 5 4 3 2 1

To Christian Donlan,
vital companion through worlds
real and imagined

CONTENTS

'What if we had a chance to do it again and again, until we finally did get it right? Wouldn't that be wonderful?'

Life After Life, KATE ATKINSON

'You've been playing for a while. Why not take a break?'

NINTENDO

Introduction

January 2012: A young man is dead and if a video game wasn't the culprit, then it was, at very least, an accessory to the crime. This wasn't the first time that a video game was a suspect in a young person's death. Thirty years earlier, almost to the month, eighteen-year-old Peter Burkowski walked into Friar Tuck's Game Room in Calumet City, Illinois, posted a high score on the arcade game *Berzerk* and, moments later, collapsed dead. Since then, fresh reports of 'death of a video gamer' (as Burkowski's story was reported at the time) have been a regular fixture in the news.

With each new story the video-game medium's reputation sinks lower. No longer is the popular charge merely that video games are a tremendous waste of time (a message that's been sustained for more than three decades, since games first emigrated from the bellies of esteemed American universities and into the local bars as *Pong* and *Space Invaders* cabinets); now they are killers too. Video games apparently take not only our young people's attention, but also, every now and again, their lives as well. And in our mortal reality, unlike that of the benevolent video game with its interminable supply of lives, there are no second chances.

The video game makes for an obvious suspect in these cautionary tales. Look at the player, sat there on the fat couch, motionless apart from the steady twitch of the hands, the unblinking eyes, the occasional grimace. This is not the lung-expanding, cheek-colouring variety of play we find on the playground or football field. It's not obviously *wholesome*. No, this appears to be an especially impoverished, depraved form of play, onanistic or, worse still, perhaps, infantile, as the controller's umbilical-like cord twirls and stretches between the human and the television screen.

Video games also destroy time. So too, of course, does a particularly engrossing novel or television drama series, but, unlike those examples, video games demand not only our full attention but also our full participation. The video game's appetite for human contact is insatiable and, as such, their detractors see them as little more than an antisocial distraction from reality and all the important stuff of life.

If nothing else, as the youngest form of art and entertainment, games are, accordingly, the least trusted. This is their inevitable lot.

Every new medium encounters similar resistance, a fear (usually generational) of change and its attendant loss, often capitalised on by the media of the time as a subject for easy sensationalism. For example, on 26 August 1858, the *San Antonio Texan* newspaper printed the following cautionary (although presumably fictional, or at least exaggerated) tale about the dangers of overindulging in novel-reading.

> A whole family brought to destitution in England, has had all its misfortunes clearly traced by the authorities to an ungovernable passion for novel reading entertained by the wife and mother. The husband was sober and industrious, but his

wife was indolent and addicted to reading everything procurable in the way of romance. This led her to utterly neglect her husband, herself and her eight children. One daughter in despair, fled the parental home, and threw herself into the haunts of vice. Another was found by the police chained by the legs to prevent her from following her sister's example. The house exhibited the most offensive appearance of filth and indigence. In the midst of this pollution, privation and poverty, the cause of it sat reading the last 'sensation work' of the season, and refused to allow herself to be disturbed in her entertainment.

Indolence, addiction, neglect, vice, filth, pollution and poverty: each noun a gavel strike aimed at the unassuming romance novel. The excerpt is echoed, if not in tone then in purpose, by contemporary newspaper articles decrying the perils of video-game addiction. Stories of video games' nefarious effects have followed the medium since its inception. In Martin Amis's non-fiction book *Invasion of the Space Invaders* we read of Anthony Hill, 'one of the more spectacular casualties of the bleeping sickness'. (Even Amis, a staunch video-game advocate at the time, employs the language of injury and disease when discussing the video game's effect on the heart and mind.) Hill was, according to Amis, an unemployed seventeen-year-old who sold sexual favours to a seventy-four-year-old pastor in exchange for money in order to fund a *Space Invaders* habit.

This was not an isolated report. In the early 1980s police in the south of England claimed that the *Space Invader* craze had 'doubled housebreaking figures'. The medium's apparent absence of virtue was debated in the English Parliament (where Hill's case was mentioned, although the boy's identity was not). On 20 May 1981 the Labour MP George Foulkes (now a baron in the House of Lords) proposed a bill for the 'Control of *Space Invaders* and Other Electronic Games' in the House of Commons. The Bill would have meant arcade and bar owners would require licences or even planning permission in order to install arcade machines for their customers. At the Bill's proposal, Foulkes said:

> 'I have seen reports from all over the country of young people becoming so addicted to these machines that they resort to theft, blackmail and vice to obtain money to satisfy their addiction. I use the word "addiction" not in its increasingly common misuse, as being generally fond of something, but in its strictly correct sense of being so attracted to an activity that all normal activity is suspended to carry it out.'

If other honourable members didn't believe Foulkes's observations, he proposed that they 'go incognito to an arcade or café in their own areas and see the effect that it is having on young people'. There they would find, he claimed, young people 'crazed, with eyes glazed, oblivious to everything around them'. He then described the profits arcade machines made as 'blood money extracted from the weakness of thousands of children'.

The following year, on 9 November 1982, US Surgeon General Dr Everett Koop gave a speech at the Western Psychiatric Institute and Clinic in Pittsburgh, in which he challenged America to confront the causes of domestic violence and child abuse. After the speech, he took a question from an audience member asking whether he thought video games had a negative effect on young people.

'Yes,' he replied. Teenagers were becoming addicted 'body and soul' to video games, a form of entertainment in which 'there's nothing constructive'.

While Foulkes's Bill did not pass (although it came preposterously close) and Dr Koop retracted his comments the day after his speech, the image of the glazed addict has persisted, even as video games have become increasingly widespread and accepted in culture. Indeed, video games have received a sustained level of popular distrust, one that their forebears in music, cinema, theatre and even print seemed to pull away from more quickly. Across the decades video games have been blamed for a multitude of crimes, from inspiring dangerous driving to being used as training devices for murderers in school shootings. Today, the president of the United States carries a laptop bearing a *Pac-Man* sticker, yet video games are still seen by many (including, I suspect, some who play them) as, if not a wholly corrupting influence, then at least a meritless time-waster.

Is that a fair appraisal?

Certainly no lives are saved, no babies delivered, no crops harvested, no cities built, no sicknesses cured, no fires extinguished, no seamen rescued, no wars won and no laws passed through the act of play. In humanity's ongoing project of survival and propagation, video games seemingly contribute little. Advocates argue that games have been shown to improve hand–eye coordination, cognitive flexibility, decision-making and even vision. Video games are increasingly sociable and inclusive. And at the philosophical level, play does, of course, educate and prepare us for usefulness in the world. But video-game play, with its abstract geometries, its fantastical dragons and its extraterrestrial threats, seems more likely to provide an escape from the roles and responsibilities of life on this side of the screen than a guide towards them.

Escapism is a powerful force. It's one of the foundations on which all literature, theatre, film and even fine art have been built: spaces into which people can retreat from the mundane familiar. But while the promise of escape might catapult humans into works of fiction, it's perhaps not enough by itself to keep them there. And if all we want is to sit back and escape, why choose a video game, with its incessant demands and tests of our competence? Far easier to lie in front of a film and let the story wash over us, unimpeded.

Why, then, do we play video games, beyond the dopamine rush of the tiny victories they afford us, or the way in which they allow us to, for a short while, step outside of ourselves and our immediate problems and circumstances? If people are dying to play video games, it's worth investigating why that might be.

As someone who has spent more than a decade writing about video games, the people who make them and the strange and curious stories that originate within and around them, I know only too well that their curious power can be difficult to explain. Game designers speak of 'compelling mechanics', of 'the play loop', of 'game balance', of 'calibrating risk and reward' and other arcane jargon. Certainly these terms and ideas can explain how games manage to keep us playing, those psychological tricks that they use to inspire compulsion. But they fail to explain the way in which video games meet our deeper, more human needs.

Death by Video Game is an investigation into a slew of deaths in which young men and, occasionally, women have been found dead at their keyboards after extended periods of video-game playing.

But we're not going to linger with the corpses. The more pressing question is what compelled these young people to emigrate from reality into their virtual dimensions beyond the natural limits of their well-being? What convinced their brains to ignore the physical warnings in order to keep playing a video game? And what, by extension, causes billions of humans around the world, those of us who don't wind up injured or dead, to revisit them week after week after week?

01

CHRONOSLIP

INSERT COIN TO CONTINUE

C hen Rong-Yu died in two places at once.

At 10 p.m. on Tuesday, 31 January 2012, the twenty-three-year-old took a seat in the farthest corner of an internet café on the outskirts of New Taipei City, Taiwan. He lit a cigarette and logged into an online video game. He played almost continuously for twenty-three hours, stopping occasionally only to rest his head on the table in front of his monitor and sleep for a little while. Each time that he woke he picked up his game where he'd left off. Then, one time, he did not raise his head. It was nine hours before a member of the café's staff tried to rouse the motionless man, in order to tell him that his time was up, only to find his body stiff and cold.

Chen Rong-yu died in two places at once. Not in the sense that during those final moments his mind drifted to another place (the landscape of some comforting memory where he might be soothed or cheered, for example). Rather, when Rong-Yu's heart failed, he simultaneously departed two realities.

He died there in the Taiwanese café, with its peeling paint and cloying heat. And he died in Summoner's Rift, a forest blanketed by perpetual gloom. Summoner's Rift has the appearance of a remote, unvisited place, but each day it is frequented by hundreds of thousands of people, players of the online video game *League of Legends*, arguably the most popular online video game in the world. Summoner's Rift is the pitch on which they do battle.

Rong-Yu had died here many times before. He had been speared, incinerated, or otherwise obliterated by rivals as he scrambled through its thickets and across its river in an endlessly repeating game of territorial warfare.

Many games are metaphors for warfare. The team sports – football, hockey, rugby and so on – are rambling battles in which attackers and defenders, led by their captains, ebb and flow up and down the field in a clash of will and power. American football is a series of frantic First World War-style scrambles for territory measured in ten-yard increments. Tennis is a pistol duel: squinting shots lined up in the glare of a high-noon sun. Running races are breakneck chases between predator and prey. Boxing doesn't even bother with the metaphor: it's a plain old fistfight ending in blood and bruise.

So it is with *League of Legends*, a game in which two teams attempt to overwhelm one another. In warfare, real or symbolic, there are inevitable casualties. To date, Rong-Yu's, deaths in the virtual forest had been symbolic and temporary, like the toppling of a pawn from a chessboard, a griefless death, easily undone. That night, however, his virtual death was mirrored in reality. It was true and final.

When the paramedics lifted Rong-Yu from his chair, his rictus hands remained in place, as if clawed atop an invisible mouse and keyboard. Like the pulp detective thriller in which the lifeless hand points towards some crucial clue, Rong-Yu's final pose appeared to incriminate his killer.

Yu's story is unusual, but not unique. On 13 July 2012, another young man, nineteen-year-old Chuang Cheng Feng, was found dead in his chair at a different Taiwanese internet café. Feng, a five-foot-five tae kwon do champion, had settled down to play the online game *Diablo 3* after a friend he was supposed to meet failed to show up. He played the game to pass the time: ten hours of uninterrupted questing. Then, mind hazed by the room's thick cigarette smoke and eyes stinging from the monitor's flicks and throbs, he decided to step outside for some fresh air.

Feng stood, took three steps then stumbled and collapsed, his mouth foaming. He too was pronounced dead at the scene.

There are others. In February 2011 a thirty-year-old Chinese man died at an internet café on the outskirts of Beijing after playing an online game for three days straight. On 2 September 2012 a forty-eight-year-old man named Liu died in Kaohsiung City following a seven-hour stint at the controller. His was the third game-related death of the year recorded in Taiwan.

In 2015 the deaths came sooner. On 1 January a thirty-eight-year-old man was found dead at an internet café in Taipei, apparently after playing video games for five days straight. A week later another: a thirty-two-year-old man, known as Hsieh, entered a café in Kaohsiung on 6 January. Two days later employees found him slumped on the desk at which he'd been playing an online game. He was pronounced dead on arrival at the hospital.

In May 2015 a man in Hefei, the largest city in the Anhui province of China, reportedly collapsed after playing a game for fourteen days straight. When the paramedics arrived, one newspaper reported him as saying, 'Leave me alone. Just put me back in my chair. I want to keep playing.'

The deaths aren't limited to South-East Asia, and they aren't only contemporary.

In April 1982 an eighteen-year-old American man, Peter Burkowski, walked into Friar Tuck's Game Room, a popular video-game arcade in Calumet City, Illinois. According to the arcade's owner, Tom Blankly, Burkowski and a friend arrived at 8.30 p.m. and began playing *Berzerk*. Burkowski was a top student who hoped to become a doctor. He also had a talent for arcade games. Within fifteen minutes he'd posted his initials next to two high scores on *Berzerk*'s leaderboard. Then he took four steps towards an adjacent machine, dropped a quarter into its slot, and collapsed dead from a heart attack.

The next day, one newspaper headline read, 'Video Game Death', the earliest report of its kind. Similar incidents have continued through the years.

In July 2011 a young British player, Chris Staniforth, died from a blood clot after a prolonged session at his Xbox video-game console.

'When Chris got into a game he could play it for hours on end,' Staniforth's father told reporters at the time. 'He got sucked in playing *Halo* online against people from all over the world. I'm not for one minute blaming the manufacturer of Xbox. It isn't their fault that people use them for so long.'

Staniforth's father absolved Microsoft, Xbox's manufacturer, and *Halo*'s publisher, of blame for his son's death. We are, he implied, each responsible for the way in which we spend our time. And yet, when Microsoft's rival Nintendo launched its Wii console, it included a warning that would interrupt many of its games. It read: 'Why not take a break?' and was accompanied by an illustration of an open window, wind blowing the curtains inwards, calling the player outside.

Nintendo knows that video games have a certain power that encourages people to inhabit an alternative reality, where time's passing goes unnoticed. The company's solution is to break the fourth wall for a moment in order to offer a way out for the spell-bound player.

The 'death by video games' story occupies a peculiar place in the modern news cycle. We don't read of 'death by cinema', 'death by literature' or 'death by crossword', even though humans must surely have died while engaged in any one of these mostly inactive pursuits. But with video games, news of a fresh tragedy arrives, usually from Asia, with grim regularity. The circumstances are always similar: a young man found dead at his keyboard, seemingly killed by an unhealthy relationship with this sedentary hobby.

For video-game players the news reports act as a cautionary tale, the kind of story mothers might tell their children to warn them off playing a hand-held game beneath the sheets after lights out: 'Look what might happen to you if you play a video game for too long.' For the newspapers, often staffed and read by a generation of people who grew up at a time when video games weren't a fixture on the cultural landscape, these tales fortify a generational distrust of the newest (and therefore most treacherous) entertainment medium.

'Gamer lies dead in internet cafe for 9 HOURS before anyone notices', wrote the *Daily Mail*'s headline writers of Rong-yu's death, with evident disapproval of the obliviousness of those who become absorbed in video games. Of course, Rong-yu's death represents a broader issue of contemporary loneliness. To be left undiscovered for more than nine hours is the kind of tragic conclusion to life that usually befalls the elderly, where the isolation of old age – the departed partner, the distant children, the dull company of daytime TV – is made explicit in death. Young people are supposed to live in vibrant company. They are supposed to be noticed when they go missing. To sit dead in a chair, in public, surrounded by people, is a news story that carries with it some of the mundane horror of contemporary life: the knowledge that, though we are packed together in cities, and through the internet, our mobile phones and online video games, and are ostensibly more connected than ever before, it's also possible to die in plain sight and for that death to go unnoticed.

This, however, was not the intended subtext of the *Daily Mail*'s story. Rather, its headline implies that, not only are video games a waste of time, not only do they encourage inactivity and obesity, not only are they used by companies to market and sell products to children, not only can they distract from work and study, they also present a mortal danger. You might die while playing them.

You could also die while sprawled out on the sofa, chain-watching the latest television serial. You might also perish after a four-hundred-page Tolstoy binge, or while you endure Abel Gance's nine-hour-long film *Napoléon*, or when caught up in an especially engaging cross-stitch pattern. People have been known to die during a twelve-hour, blood-clotting long-haul flight. Any activity that compels a human being to sit for hours on end without moving is, arguably, a mortal threat. In the 1982 Burkowski case, Mark Allen, Lake County's deputy coroner, said, sensibly, 'Peter could have died in a number of stressful situations. We once had a boy who had a heart attack while studying for an exam. It just happened that he died in front of a video game, but it's also quite interesting.'

Nevertheless, video games appear to have a better hit-rate than film, literature, exams or any of the others.

Video games, it seems, are something else.

During my first year of university, my friends and I became partially nocturnal. We'd stay up late for the 9 a.m. lectures. We'd get up early for the 9 p.m. parties. The rest of our waking hours were, as with so many students, given over to lounging in reeking halls, eating cheap pizza and playing video games. My friend Alastair provided our gateway getaway: *Goldeneye 007*, the video-game adaptation of the 1995 James Bond film. Each night (which was, for our skewed body clocks, closer to day) we'd assemble in the front room of his shared apartment, pick teams and then sprint through ancient cave systems, creep through Russian military bunkers and teeter along cranes as we shot each other in a kind of armed-combat wide game. Most nights, at around two in the morning, someone would point out that it might be time to think about ordering some food in. We'd mournfully set down the controllers and head out to the local pizza takeaway.

'Er, guys, it looks like it might be shut,' said Ian, as we rounded the corner on one such night.

'Lucky Pizza is never shut,' said Clare.

'What time is it anyway?' I asked.

'Oh,' said Alastair. 'It's half past four in the morning. How did we not notice that?'

A few years later, I left my wife playing the video game *Animal Crossing* in our apartment one afternoon.

In *Animal Crossing* you assume the role of an immigrant who moves into a rural village to build a new life. When you disembark from the train you're greeted by an officious raccoon, the local shop-owner and landlord, Tom Nook, who offers you a small house to call your own. Once you're settled in you get to know the neighbours, pen virtual letters, attend local festivals, fish, net bugs, excavate fossils, buy clothes and, of course, service your virtual mortgage. The game follows the console's internal clock and calendar: when it's night in your world, it's night in *Animal Crossing*. The shops open at nine and close at six, and Christmas falls on 25 December.

Despite the fact that talking animals populate the game and despite the fact that your work is primarily to collect fossils and catch bugs for the local museum, *Animal Crossing* mimics life's rhythms, domestic pressures and timetable.

When I returned home later that evening the flat was dark except for the quivering light of the TV screen. My partner sat on the floor, exactly as I'd left her hours earlier.

'Is everything OK?' I asked.

She turned her head stiffly, eyes hooded, as if awakening from a coma.

'Woah,' she said. 'I am cold and hungry.'

A friend of mine has coined a term for the unique way in which video games cause their players to become oblivious to time in this way: 'chronoslip'. It's not a new phenomenon. We speak of becoming 'lost in a good book', of 'losing track of time', of 'pastimes' (or, originally and more explicitly, 'passe-tymes'). The phenomenon is ancient. *Tempus fugit*, it turns out, especially while you're having fun.

But with video games, these phrases don't quite suffice. What book or movie could keep the average viewer's attention for six uninterrupted hours? The titans of modern mainstream entertainment such as *Harry Potter*, *Star Wars*, *Lord of the Rings*, *The Sopranos* et al. may boast expansive cumulative running or reading times, but they are broken into discrete, palatable chunks. With movies and TV series, we seem to reach our consumption limits sooner than with video games, into which we can descend for ceaseless hours.

Perhaps the difference is that games are active rather than passive media. They do not temporarily suppress our free will. Rather, they demand it. We step into a game world and emerge, hours later, with little sense of where the time has gone. Sometimes the immersion is so complete that our bodies' physical signals do not penetrate the unreality: we forget to eat, to shift position in our chair. We neglect to keep warm, to pee. Time becomes yoked, not to the ticking of the clock, but to the pattern of our interactions, the pleasing rhythms of cause and effect. In strategy games time is divided into the number of seconds it takes to build a barracks, train a soldier, or to mine the earth for resources. Seconds and minutes have no relevance here; time is calculated in units of action. By contrast, in a puzzle game time works like an egg timer: crack a level before your patience runs out and the timer is flipped; your store of patience is renewed.

Games achieve chronoslip because they replace the real world with a new one that moves to its own laws of physics and time.

This reality engages us totally, and we synchronise with its tempo.

Video games, from the simplest card game through to the most vividly rendered fantasy world, consume our attention. When we become lost in a book we enter a state where the fabricated world and its characters seem so real and pressing that we lose all sense of time. Small wonder it's so easy to lose oneself in a good game, where we become not only an eavesdropper or onlooker on a world, but an active participant in its action and drama. Video games go further than other fiction: they revolve around us and react to our every choice and input. Just as a piano needs a pianist or a violin needs a violinist, video games are lifeless without us. They need a player in a way that a film does not need a viewer to function.

No, video games are not mere time-wasters. This label, so often and gleefully applied, implies a certain idleness on their part. Rather, they are time-killers: they destroy time. And they are accomplished killers, often leaving little trace of their handiwork; we remain oblivious to time's passing.

Video games did not grow into the role of time-killer. They emerged, fully formed, fully capable. In his 1982 treatise on the emergent video game, *Invasion of the Space Invaders*, Martin Amis explained his first encounter with the titular Japanese arcade game, a summer romance that blossomed in a bar in the south of France during the summer of 1979.

> Now I had played quite a few bar machines in my time. I had driven toy cars, toy airplanes, toy submarines; I had shot toy cowboys, toy tanks, toy sharks. But I knew instantly that this was something different, something special. Cinematic melodrama blazing on the screen, infinite firing capacity, the beautiful responsiveness of the defending turret, the sting

and pow of the missiles, the background pulse of the quickening heartbeat ... The bar closed at eleven o'clock that night. I was the last to leave, tired but content.

Amis then describes the video-game player's descent into obsession.

Your work starts to suffer. So does your health. So does your pocket. The lies increase in frequency and daring. Anyone who has ever tangled with a drink or drug problem will know how the interior monologue goes. 'I think I've got this under control at last. It's perfectly okay so long as you do it in moderation . . .'

The addict then indulges in a wild three-hour session. 'I'm not going to touch that stuff again', he vows. Twenty minutes later he is hunched once more over the screen, giving it all his back and shoulder, wincing, gloating, his eyes lit by a galaxy of strife.

You think I exaggerate? I do but only slightly. After all, the obsession/ addiction factor is central to the game's success: you might even say that video-dependence is programmed into the computer.

The 'obsession factor' of which Amis speaks is something that is common to many types of game, not just those that are projected on a screen. The following excerpt is taken from an article entitled 'Chess-playing excitement', published in the 2 July 1859 issue of *Scientific American*.

Those who are engaged in mental pursuits should avoid a chessboard as they would an adder's nest, because chess misdirects and exhausts their intellectual energies ... It is a game which no man who depends on his trade, business or profession can afford to waste time in practicing; it is an amusement – and a very unprofitable one – which the independently wealthy alone can afford time to lose in its pursuit. As there can be no great proficiency in this intricate game without long-continued practice, which demands a great deal of time, no young man who designs to be useful in the world can prosecute it without danger to his best interests.

Like Amis, the author describes one particular player's addict-like resolution to swear off the game.

A young gentleman of our acquaintance, who had become a somewhat skillful player, recently pushed the chess-board from him at the end of the game, declaring, 'I have wasted too much time upon it already; I cannot afford to do this any longer; this is my last game.' We recommend his resolution to all those who have been foolishly led away by the present chess-excitement, as skill in this game is neither a useful nor graceful accomplishment.

In Taiwan, there have been enough café deaths that the government is no longer content with issuing mere recommendations for players to, as *Scientific American* puts it, 'make this their last game'. Government officials have developed measures to help curtail the amount of time that people play games: a more forceful kind of intervention than Nintendo's gentle reminder of the great outdoors.

According to the section chief for the Economic Development Bureau of the Tainan City Government, the police routinely carry out spot checks after 10 p.m. on cafés to see whether there are any under-eighteens on the premises. During the summer holidays the local government now runs a Youth Project, which warns young people about the dangers of playing games for too long. The government is even in the process of drafting new regulations for internet cafés that will decree when and for how long teenagers will be allowed to play on the premises. Similar legislation is already in place in South Korea where, in 2011, after a spate of similar deaths, the government introduced the Youth Protection Revision bill (sometimes known as the 'Cinderella law') which prohibits teenagers from playing online games in internet cafes after midnight.

Films are awarded age ratings that dictate the age limits of those who are allowed to view them. But video games will perhaps be the first entertainment medium in history to inspire legislation with regard to how long a person is able to interact with them before taking a break.

Amis was right: games are somehow different. We consume a book, but a game consumes us. It leaves us reeling and bewildered, hungry and ghosted in the fug of chronoslip.

The Big Net café, where Chuang Cheng Feng died, is a small business in a quiet town on the rural outskirts of Tainan. It's one of the only internet cafés in the area. Months after the incident, the owner is unwilling to talk about what happened. The death on the premises has frightened away customers, she claims, many of whom believe the cause of death was something to do with the café itself, rather than the amount of time Chuang Cheng Feng spent playing the game without interruption.

'I am afraid that recent events have been catastrophic for my business,' the café's owner tells me via a translator on the phone. 'It's suffered a huge slide. I cannot talk to you about what happened. I want us to stay out of the news now.'

Internet cafés are more widespread in Taiwan than in the West.

For young players it's more economical to play games at one of these establishments than at home. Two dollars buys eight hours of game time. Take into account the cost of a broadband connection, a PC, electricity and the games themselves, and an internet café is the most affordable location in which to play an online game.

Big City is one of the larger café franchises in Taiwan. I call a branch in the Yongkang District of Tainan, fifteen miles from the café where Feng died.

'Yeah, since the news of that death, business has been different,' says Lian, the twenty-five-year-old staff member who answers the phone. 'It's far quieter than usual. It seems probable to me that this downturn is somehow linked.'

'Are you worried that the same thing that happened in Yujing might happen in your café?' I ask.

'Of course,' she says.

'Have you taken any measures to prevent a similar tragedy?'

'Headquarters held a meeting after Feng's death,' Lian says. 'After that, employees were issued with new guidelines, asking us to pay closer attention to customers. We have been told to issue a verbal warning if we notice any customer sitting at the same terminal for too long. To be honest, though, I haven't noticed anyone behaving in the same manner as Feng did.'

A little farther north, twenty-seven-year-old Huang, branch manager of the Ingame Café, is more willing to admit that people playing games for prolonged periods of time is an issue.

'Our business has been mostly unaffected by the recent death,' she says. 'We do have customers like that, who stay here for a very long time. Not many, but certainly a few. But I'm not really worried that something like that might ever happen here. We have a system to prevent customers from sitting in front of the computer for too long.'

'How long is too long?' I ask.

'We don't allow any customers to play for more than three days at a time. Once it gets past that amount of time we ask the customer to go home, rest and refresh. This is a well-organised internet café, you see.'

She pauses for a moment. 'You know what? Don't even mention three days. In fact, I just asked a customer to leave who had been here for over twenty-four hours.'

'Why?' I say. 'Was there a problem?'

'Other customers had started to complain about his smell. So I asked him to leave. In my experience, no one tends to play a game for longer than a day and a half at a time.'

When it comes to apportioning blame for the deaths of Rong-Yu, Feng and all the others, Miss Huang is unequivocal.

'The problem with this sort of addiction stems from those addicts themselves,' she says. 'It's probably their family or their education that's to blame. It's really a matter of self-discipline.'

Since the 1970s doctors have believed that it's possible for a video game to trigger a heart attack in a person with a weak heart. In 1977 the cardiologist Robert S. Eliot used *Pong* to replicate stressful situations for his cardiac patients at the University of Nebraska Medical Center. He studied more than one thousand patients, monitoring the game's effect on their heart rate and blood pressure.

'We have had heart rate increases of sixty beats per minute and blood pressures as high as 220 within one minute of starting a computer game,' he said at the time. 'It happens quite a lot but the patients have no awareness.'

In fact, Peter Burkowski's autopsy in 1982 found that the young man had scar tissue on his heart that was at least two weeks old. The coroner recorded that the stress of the arcade games Burkowski had been playing triggered the attack in his weakened heart, lending credence to Dr Eliot's claims.

If Rong-yu's death was, as Miss Huang believes, a failing of self-discipline or some other non-biological defect, then it's important to establish that his heart attack wasn't due to a pre-existing medical condition.

Dr Ta-Chen Su is the attending physician and clinical associate professor at the Department of Internal Medicine, National Taiwan University Hospital. The number of cases of young men dying while playing games is too few to have inspired any specific research into the phenomenon. But Su has a personal interest in the subject: Rong-Yu was his patient.

The NTUH is housed in a grand redbrick building, fronted by pairs of Doric columns that bite into the pavement by the side of a Taipei main road. Outside, the oily scent of traffic hangs in the air, while the interior is all disinfectant and white fluorescent lighting.

'It wasn't reported, but last year Chen had a heart attack and was transferred to the hospital for evaluation,' Dr Su tells me. 'During his hospitalisation the checks included echocardiography, twenty-four-hour electrocardiography, cardiac catheterization, coronary angiography and cardiac electrophysiology.'

But the test results showed no signs that Rong-Yu had a heart problem that might lead to sudden death. The young man's unexpected heart attack was something of a mystery. Rong-Yu refused the doctor's recommendation to have a cardioverter-defibrillator fitted. Moreover, when he discovered that there was nothing wrong with his heart, he declined to have any more cardiovascular tracking, which might have explained the attack. Three months later Rong-Yu was dead.

'As we can eliminate any pre-existing heart problems from his cause of death, he must have died from another cause,' says Su.

Dr Su believes that there are multiple possible causes of death for Rong-Yu, as for the other people who have died while playing video games in internet cafés.

'Acute autonomic dysfunction is the first potential cause of death,' he says. 'Video games can generate a great deal of tension in the human body. The player's blood pressure and heart rate rise. If this excessive tension is maintained for more then ten hours, it can result in cardiac arrhythmia and sympathetic-parasympathetic imbalance, also called acute autonomic dysfunction.'

Video games deal in tension and peril. This is true of most fiction, in which conflict is necessary to create drama, but in most video games the player is the subject of the stress and conflict. The conflict is necessary for the sense of triumph, release and learning that comes when it's overcome. But Dr Su warns that this cycle of stress and release, when prolonged, can have physiological effects.

'Even if the game is not especially stressful in this way, simply playing for such a long period of time can prove fatal,' he adds.

Dr Su compares playing games for days at a time to putting in unhealthy amounts of overtime at work – something that leads to exhaustion of the mind and body.

In Japan, enough people have died at their desks while working overtime that the Japanese invented the term *karōshi*, or death by overwork. In 1987 the Japanese Ministry of Labour even began to publish statistics on *karōshi*. The International Labour Organization (ILO), a United Nations agency that deals with labour issues, has published an article on the phenomenon, warning that all-night, late-night or holiday work for long and excessive hours can lead to a worker's death. If death at the workstation is a frequent and well-documented occurrence, then death at the PlayStation appears to be the flipside of the same coin.

The third potential cause of Rong-yu's death, according to Dr Su, is what doctors refer to as 'Economy Class Syndrome'.

'Many studies show that maintaining the same pose for hours at a time without moving your body, especially your legs, can cause deep vein thrombosis,' he explains. 'Moreover, if you don't drink and eat properly while in this position, your blood can become sticky, leading to a pulmonary embolism and sudden death.'

The final potential cause of death is linked to the cafés themselves, specifically their conditions. Taiwanese internet cafés typically have poor ventilation and offer players only a cramped space to play in. One recent study found that the air pollution index in internet cafés often exceeds safe levels. Most establishments have dedicated smoking zones on the premises, but while air conditioners cool the air temperature, they don't improve its quality.

Taiwan in particular is a humid country. Relative humidity usually remains at 60 to 90 per cent, conditions that help fungi, bacteria and dust mites to flourish in a confined space. According to Dr Su, these can stimulate asthma and other allergic syndromes. Severe air pollution can have a devastating impact on a human's heart and blood vessels, increasing the possibility of blood clots, raising the heart rate and blood pressure, stiffening the arteries and having a negative impact on haemodynamics.

None of this explains the apparent rise in these deaths, however.

'It's because more and more internet cafés are opening and the number of people taking up online gaming is increasing,' says Dr Su. 'The content of online gaming is improving and growing more attractive than ever. I believe that, if café conditions don't change, we are going to see more deaths.'

Rong-yu's death is a whodunnit of sorts. It's not a crime that can be easily pinned on any one person or thing. There's Taiwan's local economy and infrastructure, which promotes the extended use of internet cafés. There are the natural conditions of the country's humid climate. There's the lack of regulation with regard to how long people can use these cafés and, of course, there are the video games themselves, which promote prolonged engagement through their elegant, compelling design, often iterated upon hundreds of times to inspire humans to willingly offer their uninterrupted attendance and attention.

But there is another, more pressing, more interesting question that arches over all of these, one that is, perhaps, more relevant to the billions of people around the world who play video games and don't wind up dead from doing so: whydunnit?

What is it about this medium that encourages some people to play games to the extremes of their physical well-being and beyond? Why do video games inspire such monumental acts of obsession? Is it something within the game's reality that proves so appealing, or is it external circumstances that push certain people to take refuge in a cosy unreality?

Games offer conflict within safe bounds, so perhaps it is to do with the human desire to be heroic, to perform acts for which they might be remembered, a way to stave off death's great whitewash.

Or is it the competitiveness of the athlete: the desire to win and assert dominance over our peers and rivals? Or is it to do with friendship and community, or showboating and braggadocio?

Video games offer the intrigue and joy of solvable mysteries. They also grant access to mysterious places in need of discovery. Through them we have the opportunity to, like our ancestors, become explorers when Google satellites have mapped every inch of our own world, leaving few places where we can truly explore the unseen.

Glory, justice, immortality; a chance to live over and again in order to perfect our path, a place in which change and growth in us are measured in the irrefutable high-score table. Video games offer all of this and more. The allures of the video game, and the ways in which it salves our internal problems and instincts, are myriad.

Is it so curious that a person might become forever lost in this rift between the real and the unreal?

02

SUCCESS

INSERT COIN TO CONTINUE

It's 11 o'clock on a Saturday night and London's drunk.

She gets like this from time to time, usually at the weekend. Sometimes the booze manifests itself in shouts and swagger, in fistfights spewed out through bar doors onto the pavement. Tonight, though, the city's wrapped in a gentle sort of inebriation, an exaggerated swaying on the train ride home, eyes clenched shut with concentration: down stomach, down.

The Trocadero, one of the capital's few remaining amusement arcades, is a short walk from Piccadilly Circus's bright lights and slogans. A hen party, all crooked tiaras and bleared mascara, totters past the giant double doors: these stretched escalators and polished floors are no place for cocktails on high heels. Inside, rows of arcade machines buzz and bleep, attract mode sequences beckoning the curious with the promise of pixel adventure. Teenagers stand idly by with a studied nonchalance. They glance at player performances here and there with self-conscious dispassion.

Arcades like this are video gaming's public installations, a shared focal point for performance and drama in front of an impromptu assembled audience. It was in such a venue that the medium made its public debut when Atari founder Nolan Bushnell installed his first arcade cabinet, *Computer Space*, in the Dutch Goose bar near Stanford University in 1971. The video game – a homeless invention that previously never had a natural location to call its own – flourished in public. A year after *Computer Space*'s arrival Al Acorn, one of Atari's first employees, was called to Andy Capp's Tavern in Sunnyvale, California, where a *Pong* location test machine had malfunctioned. On arrival Acorn opened the coin box to issue himself free credits for testing, only to be showered with coins. The game had proved so popular that the coin mechanism had seized.

The moneymaking heyday is gone. Video-game arcades are dismissed by most as relics of a bygone era, a pastime that has little relevance to the medium's contemporary landscape. In a sense that's true. The value of the arcade was, for many, in providing a road map to interactive technology's future, a sparkling promo for the destinations to which home-based video games would arrive in a few years' time. Then, as console manufacturers closed that technological gap, it grew more difficult to draw players from the comfort of their homes. People didn't get out so much, when it came to video games. Today arcades have mostly vanished, the industry that fathered video games mostly forgotten by young players.

The tragedy is that arcades came to symbolise technical prowess. This focus became their destruction, because it ignored their true power and appeal, their ability to bring a crowd together to watch a masterly performance. Video games are closer to music than film in this regard. Games and music both allow their performers to interpret the experience that the creator devised, adding personal inflections and character to make the piece their own. They allow their players to accent, to flex, to showboat, to be virtuoso. In this sense arcades were the public venues for video-game performance, where a skilled player could show off their talent to a watching crowd.

Upstairs, to the right of the central escalator that runs like a spinal column up from the Trocadero's entrance to the building's summit, there is a *Dance Dance Revolution* cabinet. First released in 1998, this is a game that's played not with one's fingers and thumbs, but with one's feet. Players must step in time with the music that blares from the machine's speakers, pressing down on one of four arrows on the floor in front of the cabinet, copying the on-screen directions as if reading a formative kind of musical notation. The premise is simple, but mastery is hard won. Everyone's first time with the game descends into an awkward tussle of limbs, partly hilarious, partly humiliating. The muscle memory required to conquer the streams of directional inputs extends across one's whole body – and until you have built the necessary skills, it's easy to trip over your feet and end up in a heap on the floor.

In London the machine still holds pride of place, dominating the scene with its bulk and noise. The coin mechanism is yet to jam from overuse, but it must still be the operator's highest-earning machine to warrant such a valuable location.

On this particular night a crowd of teenagers and young twenty-somethings loiter around the machine. They are not here to play. They are here to perform and to be performed to. The rows of teenagers ripple out from the spectacle at their centre, eyes fixed on the two alpha teens perched with their elbows on the machine's rest bars. As the flurry of beats stabs the air through the machine's oversized speakers, their legs spasm, bodies twisting in staccato rhythm with the game's directional arrows. The game judges their rhythmic timing with on-screen pronouncements: 'Perfect', 'Perfect', 'Very Good', 'Perfect'. It might not be dancing in the strict sense – more foot-controlled Simon Says – but it dazzles.

The song ends with the crack of a processed snare, and both men step down from the platform, sweating and exhaling but also smirking at their accomplishment and, more importantly, the attention their performance has received. Both walk away with a kind of slow-motion bluster, seeking to hide any trace of exertion, pretending this is the most natural thing in the world and what-the-hell-are-you-staring-at-anyway?

Now a short, plump man in his late thirties steps forward. He wears tight jeans crowned by a bright orange bum-bag slung over his hip: a holster for the tools of tourism containing, presumably, camera, hotel key card and passport.

His walk is affected, as if he's trying to blend with the group around him, but his awkwardness betrays his otherness. There is an audible inhalation from the crowd as he adds his coin to the line of game reservations resting at the bottom of the screen. Spectators' eyes meet for the first time: is this guy for real?

Five minutes later, it is his turn. He steps to the platform with a heavy foot and the buzz rises in intensity, the crowd all whisper and jostle.

In *Dance Dance Revolution* there are a number of ways you can play. The most straightforward is 'single', during which you step in time to the music over just the four directional arrows of a compass. Up, down, left and right. There is space on the platform for two players to do this simultaneously, playing side by side against each other, each on their own four-arrowed section. For those who are exceptionally talented, rehearsed or naive, it is possible to play 'double', whereby you must step complicated patterns over both sides of the platform, with no fewer than eight potential positions for your feet, as if performing the dances of two people simultaneously. In this scenario the rhythmic shower of directional commands snakes across the machine, and the whole exercise becomes much more physical as players must move their body across a wider area in an effort to hit the pads in sequence.

As the man selects to play across both sets of pads on the game's toughest song the crowd's buzz carries a single question: is this man talented or rash? More than half the watchers presume he's blindly picking options that he doesn't understand. No one considers the truth: this fumbling, pausing and scratching-of-head is a kind of pantomime, baiting the audience for a switch that will happen seconds later as he finally begins to dance.

For the next eight or so minutes the crowd watches agog, immovable, exchanging smiles, nods and head-shaking disbelief with each other. The dancer never misses a beat. 'Perfect', 'Perfect', 'Perfect'. Then, at the climax of his performance, the man, glistening and portly, jumps from the machine with a slim smile and tears off down the escalator.

The crowd dissipates into the cold night outside, smiling to itself, drunk on wonder.

Dance Dance Revolution makes the performative aspect of video games obvious. As its player twists and taps in time with the music, their skill is as evident as that of the leaping athlete (and, like the athlete or musician, *Dance Dance Revolution* masters are not born but made; they too must rehearse and practise behind closed doors, acquiring the muscle memory and technique). But, like any video game that scores its player on their performance, *Dance Dance Revolution* has an element of competition. The high-score table, which ranks players according to their best performance, acts like a thrown gauntlet: play me, get good and, just maybe, your name will be recorded here, among the greats. Video games, in their scores, levels and trophies, offer a neat numerical read-out of a person's skill, effort and achievement. Progress and improvement can be measured cleanly and clearly, as you top the rankings in a *Call of Duty* match or reach the next level in *Space Invaders*. And on this battlefield you are able to compete for hours without physically tiring as you might in a game of football.

The thrill of video-game competition and the quest for glory are what draws millions of players into online video games each day, and keeps them coming back. They've been present and enduring since the medium's emergence.

Founded in 2004 in a former metal shop at 388 Union Avenue, Brooklyn, Barcade is an establishment that expresses its gimmickry through its name with rare economy: a bar themed around 1980s arcade machines. Barcade has little of the grime and grubbiness of its New York amusement arcade forerunners, whose players would hunch like addicts, swapping tips in whispers as they competed for high-score dominance some twenty-five years ago. For Barcade's patrons, most of whom are in their twenties, this is, rather, a museum of outmoded technology.

They wear much the same uniform as their forebears: Martin Amis, following his dalliance with an arcade machine in southern France, moved to New York, where he described the wardrobe of the average arcade-goer at the time as: 'woolly hat, earphones, windbreaker, jeans, moonboots and a Rubik's Cube key-ring', a similar uniform to that of the twenty-first-century Williamsburg hipster. But the majority of today's clientele come to enjoy the ambiance rather than feed a high-score-chasing habit. They come for this parade of hands-on exhibits, curios whose bleeps and flashes provide an atmospheric link to a past long gone but, through the iconography of *Space Invaders* and *Pac-Man*, not forgotten, and even made fashionable. (The chunky pixel aesthetic of 1980s video games is again popular, this time not through technological necessity, but through artistic choice. Many game developers use archaic pixel art as an aesthetic, either to infuse their game with an air of nostalgia, or simply because they prefer to work with these cartoonish sprites.)

Regardless of the *zeitgeist* that gathered these machines today, there's something transporting about their physicality. Stare into the *Asteroid* field, face lit up white and fixed five inches from the screen, and the experience is no less mesmerising than when it rolled out of designer Ed Logg's mind and into bars in 1979. Barcade offers a glimpse of how things once were, when the video-game industry was still in its mewling infancy. Grasp an arcade stick here and you shake hands with one of the medium's proto-Adams, that which begat *Galaxian*, which begat *Defender*, which begat *Elite*, which begat *Super Mario World*. Here you can reconnect with that past.

Then there are those who come here not for nostalgia, or for a beery lesson in interactive history. Rather, they come for something else, something more alive and current. Because here, in the monolithic permanence of the high-score table (many of which still proudly display the three-letter initials of players who recorded their scores in years gone by), some of the video-game form's primal appeal can be found.

Hank Chien is a plastic surgeon from New York. He specialises in reshaping his patients' eyes to create a crease in the upper eyelid. He first heard about Barcade when browsing the *Donkey Kong* world leaderboard, an online list of the highest scores ever recorded on the formative arcade game. Unlike other patrons, he comes to Barcade not to soak up the beer and atmosphere, but to compete.

A few months before he found the global *Donkey Kong* leaderboard Chien had watched the Seth Gordon documentary *King of Kong*, a film that documents the rivalry between two of the arcade game's best players, Billy Mitchell and Steve Wiebe, as they compete for the world record score in the game. Chien, curious about the game (he was seven when it originally launched in 1981; the Taiwanese national had never played it before), loaded a version onto his home computer only to discover a natural, latent talent for the game. Each night when he returned home from his private practice in Flushing, Queens, he would play *Donkey Kong*.

Donkey Kong was the first video game designed by the medium's most famous and storied designer, Shigeru Miyamoto, shortly after he joined Nintendo in the mid-1970s as an artist. Initially the young designer was told to devise a game featuring the cartoon character Popeye. Nintendo, however, was unable to obtain the rights to the American comic strip so Miyamoto was instead asked to invent his own character for the game. Drawing inspiration from the classic 1933 film *King Kong* and the fable *Beauty and the Beast*, he constructed a simple story involving a gorilla that had escaped from its cage and kidnapped the player character's girlfriend, Pauline. In the story, the gorilla climbed to the top of a seven-storey construction site and began hurling barrels at his pursuer below.

Nintendo's president, Hiroshi Yamauchi, asked Miyamoto to choose an English name for the game. Miyamoto used a dictionary to look up the words he wanted: 'Donkey', as a synonym for 'Stubborn', and 'Kong' for gorilla. The gorilla's master, the player-character, was just known as 'Jumpman'.

The game was a sizeable success and sold more than 67,000 machines in the US. Following the success, Nintendo changed Jumpman's name to Mario in honour of the company's US landlord, Mario Segale, who had generously agreed to give the company's American office more time to pay its rent prior to *Donkey Kong*'s release. Super Mario was born.

The game's vital place in the medium's history is clear, but its success was no fluke. *Donkey Kong* has endured not only for its memorable characters (and a high-profile legal case brought by the film studio Universal, which claimed the game was based on its seminal film *King Kong*) but for its allure as a competitive game, a place where players are able to showboat and quest for glory, competing against both the titular ape and other players who seek to demonstrate their dominance through the high-score table's resolute verdict.

Chien grew up in Forest Hills, Queens, and attended Stuyvesant High School and then Harvard, where he was a maths and computer science major. He graduated from the Mt Sinai School of Medicine. *Donkey Kong* quickly became the ideal way for the young doctor to relax, even though the precise twitches and jolts of play mimicked his day job.

The surgeon soon realised he had a talent for the game. After three months of concerted effort, he managed to reach the 'kill screen', a notorious threshold for any player of the game: the point at which *Donkey Kong* freezes owing to a programming bug, after which it is impossible to progress.

Eager to take his new-found talent on the road, but unsure of where he might find a working *Donkey Kong* cabinet in the wild, Chien logged on to the internet and visited Twin Galaxies, a Guinness World Records-endorsed website that collates the world's highest recorded scores for a slew of arcade games. Chien wanted to know whether there was another top-flight *Donkey Kong* player in New York, someone with whom he might share tips and secrets and, if he got lucky, someone who owned a working cabinet on which he could practise. Almost immediately Chien found his man: Benjamin Falls, one of the top *Donkey Kong* players in the world.

'I contacted him through the site and we immediately became friends,' Chien tells me. 'Now I would consider him a mentor to me.' Falls introduced his new protégé to a number of other top *Donkey Kong* players. They invited him to Barcade, the only bar in New York with a working *Donkey Kong* cabinet.

'Naturally *Donkey Kong* was the first game I played on my initial visit,' says Chien. 'What grabbed me about the game were the constant improvements in your scores and the long learning curve. No matter how good you are, there are always ways to improve your game.' *Donkey Kong* also appealed to Chien as it's a game that dynamically creates its challenge. Players have to learn its concepts, rather than merely memorising the precise moments at which to jump. 'People talk about patterns in *Donkey Kong* when really they are just guidelines,' he says. 'There are no patterns in *Donkey Kong*, and the ones people refer to as patterns frequently fall apart.'

After another few months of playing at Barcade under the tutelage of more experienced players, Chien was able to reach the kill screen consistently. 'At that point, I decided I would buy my own machine, record a score, submit it to Twin Galaxies, sell my machine and be done,' he says. 'However, I was still improving, and by the time I got my machine I wanted more than to merely reach the kill screen: I wanted a million points. At the time there were only two official scores in excess of a million points so it was an ambitious goal.'

The first time Hank Chien broke a million points, he was killing time in his small apartment in midtown Manhattan before a flight. It was a victory but, somehow, it didn't satisfy in the way that he had hoped. He had reached his ambitious goal but, with all the drawn-eyed hunger of the glory addict, he decided it wasn't enough; he wanted more.

Chien had his chance to improve upon his feat a few weeks later, in February 2010, when a snowstorm forced him to cancel his surgery schedule for the day, allowing him to sleep in.

'I actually tried to go to work that day,' he recalls. 'When I reached my car, it was engulfed in snow up to the side-view mirrors. I called my office and cancelled everything for the day. Being locked at home, I decided to make some world record attempts.'

Chien switched on the *Donkey Kong* cabinet that stands next to his television. At first found he 'couldn't get a game started', as he puts it. The game's first few levels are more random than those that follow, and frequently players will take more risks since the stakes are lower. 'This is why you'll see even the top players dying very often in the early stages and sometimes taking hours before they play out a game,' says Chien. 'I took frequent breaks and caught up on sleep throughout the day.'

That night, well rested and relaxed, Chien sat down for a final attempt of the day. Two and a half hours later, moments after the strike of midnight, Chien stood to his feet, shouting the proclamation: 'New world record!'

'It is a good feeling to know you're the best in the world at something,' Chien told the *New York Times* shortly after his victory, 'but one thing about *Donkey Kong*, you know there are people out there trying every day to break your record.' Indeed, Billy Mitchell, the previous record holder, wrested the title back five months later with a score of 1,062,800 points. Steve Wiebe, the other major *Donkey Kong* competitor who was featured in Gordon's film, set a new record with a score of 1,064,500 points the following month. Then, in February 2011, Chien set another world record at the Funspot arcade in New Hampshire. This rapid leap-frogging demonstrates the vibrancy of competition within the game, the draw for competitors to prove their dominance at a game that, in technological terms at least, has been outmoded for decades.

The quest for glory through the wager of public performance has always been a part of the video game's appeal. Video games *are* like musical instruments, but that is only half of the truth. They are also very often like sports, constantly appraising the player's performance in words or numbers. They are competitive, driving players to strive for domination. They are a challenge, and one that most obviously accounts for the acts of human obsession and commitment to their simulated bounds, even, as in *Donkey Kong*'s case, decades after their debut. For many players, video games offer the same thrill and appeal as sports: an opportunity to prove oneself, to measure oneself against others, a focal point for aggression, rivalry and battle within a simulated domain.

This would have been a significant factor in keeping Chen Rong-Yu at his keyboard the night that he died. *League of Legends*, the game that Rong-Yu was playing, is so effective at drawing its players into the cycle of sport and improvement that there are now training houses around the world whose residents live together only to improve at *League of Legends*.

One such group lives and practises less than an hour's drive from the internet café in which Rong-Yu died.

The Taipei101 skyscraper's stratospheric tendrils stab at the Chinese capital's skyline. This was the first building to break the half-kilometre mark, its towering silhouette an exclamation point to mark modern man's obsession and achievement. The 101 floors inside provide office space to many of the world's largest investment banks and corporations, including Google and Starbucks. It's filled with the pungent aromas of money, success. The surrounding area is some of Taipei's most expensive real estate, home to well-to-do bankers, lawyers; it's a seat for the city's mayor.

It's also home to five young men who, in 2012, left their homes and moved into a penthouse apartment within the Taipei101's shadow. The friends are unlikely neighbours to the other Xinyi

District residents. They don't have high-powered jobs in industry or technology and, at the time they moved in at least, none could be considered rich.

Chen, Alex, Stanley, Toyz and Bebe are the Taipei Assassins, a professional eSports team who, for two years, used this spacious house as their headquarters, home and training facility.

In January 2012 the training began in earnest. The days started at 9 a.m. and lasted for thirteen hours. During this time the young men played *League of Legends* almost continuously, trying out new techniques, then refining them, watching replays of their mistakes and victories and poring over footage of other teams' matches in an effort to discern their rivals' idiosyncrasies, strengths and weaknesses.

'TPA', as its fans would later affectionately refer to the team, spent two hours each day exercising and taking English classes; an education to produce a PR burnish. This dual focus on inward and outward professionalism was no coincidence: Garena, a private company based in Singapore, paid for the house, its twenty computers, food and weekly cleaners. Garena's directors hoped that their investment might be recouped in tournament winnings.

On 13 October 2012, in front of eight million viewers at the Los Angeles Galen Center, the gamble paid off: the Taipei Assassins won the *League of Legends* world championship final. Their winnings totalled $1 million.

So-called 'gaming houses' are not a new idea, Michael O'Dell, manager of Dignitas, one of the oldest and largest professional eSports teams in the world, tells me.

'Since the very first professional video-game tournaments I became involved with in the early 2000s, teams have lived together in order to spend more time practising,' he says. 'Although I suppose until recently they functioned more like a boot camp before a large tournament – a few weeks of intense training in hired accommodation.'

Today, gaming houses are year-round arrangements, perennial exercise camps for professional young teams to train in, away from distraction.

'Living together changes everything,' says O'Dell. 'When my teams practise remotely over the internet I don't know what's going on in the background. Are they concentrating properly? Is the television on? Is the girlfriend there interfering? But when you're in a gaming house – especially when you have a manager and an analyst there with you, looking over your shoulder – nobody's mucking around. They're fully focused.'

eSports – the business of professional competitive video-game playing – is still in its infancy. But what has been something of a cultural sideshow has begun to grow into a major commercial concern, fuelled by corporations such as Garena, who scout and hire talented young players, provide them with food and a dedicated training facility and, naturally, take a healthy cut of any winnings (O'Dell: 'The team receive the majority of the prize money in the event of a win; but of course we take a cut too'). The first *League of Legends* grand prize amounted to $50,000. In 2012 that grew to $1 million and, in 2014, was more than $2 million. As the size of the prizes increases so too does the professionalism and dedication of the competitors and the interest of the entrepreneurial businessmen who support them. Money changes sport, even virtual sport.

Dignitas now employs seventy players in eighteen different countries around the world, all managed by O'Dell from his home office in Surrey, England. Each player on the team earns a basic salary of $25,000 a year, but this can increase drastically with sponsorship deals and winnings. The multimillion-dollar prize pots make attractive headlines for young game players. But the steady salaries offer a chance to turn a hobby into a profession.

'Last year we decided to rent a house full time and do it properly,' says O'Dell. 'A gaming house is where the players live and train so they think about the game 24/7. It makes everything more cohesive.' Initially O'Dell settled upon a large house in Beverly Hills, close to Hugh Hefner's Playboy Mansion. But when the team moved in they found that the landlord had exaggerated the speed of the internet connection. In online eSports, a house's network connection speed is a far more important selling point than a spacious kitchen or downstairs bathroom.

The team broke off the contract with the landlord and, after a few weeks' searching, settled upon another extravagant mansion, this time overlooking Long Beach, California.

'We wanted a gated community and somewhere pretty remote,' says O'Dell. Why did the house need to be remote? 'Because the team has got a hell of a lot of fans. We didn't want them being distracted all of the time. That said: we've already had a couple of people find out where they're based and come knocking.'

Riot Games, *League of Legends*' developer, is intimately involved with these teams. Indeed, in many cases the studio is directly paying for their houses. For the makers of competitive video games, a vibrant eSports league is a key ingredient in a game's potential success, bringing a different sort of profile, interest and drama to the game.

'A healthy league is a great asset to the developer and builds interest in their game,' explains O'Dell, 'but it also adds an element of aspiration for many fans.' Brandon Beck, Riot's founder, admits the studio was reluctant to turn its game into a sport: 'We never fancied ourselves as league commissioners,' he says. 'I don't think it was on anyone's Top 50 list of things they wanted to do – it's not a core competency of any game developer. But we get it. When you're creating a professional sport it's part of the job.'

For this reason, in 2013 Riot began paying each of the top professional teams a salary, thereby ensuring that no player ducks out mid-season owing to failing interest or team squabbling, legitimate risks in a sport populated by relative youngsters (Dignitas's five *League of Legends* players range in age from nineteen to just twenty-three). Combined rent and bills on the team Dignitas house is around $5,500 per month, most of which is paid for by Riot. It's no great surprise. This sort of property is out of the price range of most people of their age. Indeed, for many players in the league who have moved into gaming houses, it's the first time they've lived away from their parents.

Despite the players' youth there's little in the way of carousing for these devotees.

'Our guys are not party animals,' O'Dell says. 'They are professional. They know that this is a training camp. They know what they are playing for.' With so much money at stake, small wonder the team skips partying. 'Anyone who doesn't take it seriously is crazy,' O'Dell says. 'In my mind there's no difference to a professional sport. You have to make sacrifices to be the best. That's what these guys do. And they get paid a lot of money to do it.'

Ostensibly, gaming houses are about a sport (or, perhaps, a hobby with ambitions to become a sport) beginning to take itself more seriously. Footage of the occupants' daily routine may make for an uninspiring training montage in a sports movie – the grim clicking in front of the milky glow of a screen, surrounded by a shanty town of headphones and fast-food cartons – but the aim is shared with traditional athletes: to close out the world in order to fully focus on one's chosen talent.

More generally and perhaps more pertinently, gaming houses are about a sport beginning to be taken more seriously. In July 2013 O'Dell hired an immigration lawyer who successfully campaigned to have one of Dignitas's players issued with a US athlete visa, a move that effectively sees the game recognised as a professional sport. For the managers that pull the teams together and pay for their lodgings and the developers who organise the championships in which they participate, gaming houses are a way to legitimise or formalise a sport that might otherwise appear to be transient and of-a-moment. These residences offer a badge of authenticity scrawled onto the landscape: look, they proclaim, we have training facilities just like the real sports. We, like bricks and mortar, are here to stay.

It's telling that the gaming house's purpose is, in no small part, to ensure that the young players don't quit a league mid-season, distracted by any one of the scores of tantalising teenage diversions. These are, after all, not young athletes who have worked their way up through clubs, sacrificing weekends at the gym or grimly practising in harsh weather. They are video-game players, who discovered that they could click and blink more quickly than their rivals. For all the spectacle, the silver championship cups, the inconceivably large online viewerships (in 2014 the *Wall Street Journal* reported that Twitch, a website that broadcasts online eSports matches, accounts for more US internet traffic during peak usage hours than any other company apart from Netflix, Google and Apple) and the money-spinning corporate sponsorships, eSports wears its name awkwardly. A day's work that begins at 1 p.m. and ends at 10 p.m. might be considered gruelling to an adolescent, fatigued by hormones and growth, but it's hardly the schedule of the athlete.

Nevertheless, O'Dell views his team as sportsmen and the game as a sport just like any other. Team Dignitas has around sixty players, who play across nine different video games. More than half of them draw a salary, derived from tournament winnings, sponsorship deals and, most recently, advertising revenue earned from Twitch. The best players can earn up to $200,000 a year (O'Dell estimates the average annual salary is currently around $60,000). With so much at stake, he has hired a life coach to spend time with his players.

'They're able to open up to him about their problems, both personal and professional,' he says. 'Last week he took them to the beach and they built sandcastles together as a team-building exercise. It has to be like a family, a team, otherwise it doesn't work at all.'

The recent rise of gaming houses emphasises the sport-like aspects of the medium. But they're not necessarily a poor cousin to football, tennis et al. Video games have added advantages over traditional sports. They are regulated and refereed by an omniscient and fair computer. There is no doubt over whether a goal was in or not, or whether one player fouled another. It's all there, in the watching code, which guarantees unimpeachable fairness (indeed, professional sports increasingly rely on computerised referees). Secondly, they do not demand physical fitness or prowess. Sure, the nippy reactions of youth offer an advantage, but video games are a sedentary pursuit. They offer all of the psychological benefits of sport – the excitement, the fervour, the racing pulse, the strategy – without the lactic acid chaser. Indeed, for a certain type of person, a video game can be played almost indefinitely without the need for rest or interruption.

This is their great benefit, but it's also their great peril. For some people, devotion to improving at a video game begins to mimic the unbreakable grip of substance addiction, if not the chemical dependence.

Matthew Boyle began playing the online role-playing game *World of Warcraft* when he was nineteen years old and working a night shift in a factory. At first playing the game was a hobby, a way to pass the afternoons before he left for work. But when Boyle lost his job the focus changed.

'I didn't go balls-to-the-wall right away,' he says, 'but I did become severely addicted. The real transition happened when the exploration and thrill of this new world faded. Now the goal was to become better than the next person.'

It was the friend who first introduced Boyle to *World of Warcraft* who taught him a more 'hardcore' way of playing. 'We were on a levelling binge,' he says, 'and instead of taking turns playing we would take turns sleeping. After that the average day involved waking up to log in, and playing till I couldn't stay awake any longer. Sometimes this went on for days at a time till I'd fall asleep in a puddle of drool, and wake up with a waffle print in my face from the keyboard.'

Boyle's impoverished circumstances fuelled his interest in the game. He had no job, a 'horrible girlfriend' and a 'slum of an apartment' with no heating or windows. 'I would skip showers because the place was so horrendously cold,' he recalls. 'I'd rather deal with the discomfort of being filthy. But in the game I was in the top five hundred players worldwide. I was a success. So there was more of a motivation to better my avatar and go for numbers in rankings than there was to further my education. When achieving an ultra-hard kill, or getting rare loot, I could only compare that feeling to what I would assume achieving something great within a team might feel like.'

Justin Edmond, another self-professed 'powergamer', also plays *World of Warcraft* with the focus and enthusiasm of an employee working for a promotion. 'At first I started playing *World of*

Warcraft with the sole aim of the final boss at the time,' he tells me. 'Killing him was such a huge event: we had tried for weeks and when he finally dropped I screamed in excitement. After that it was a case of trying to recreate that thrill.'

Edmond, who lives in Alberta, USA, and his friends attempted to recreate the thrill by chasing 'world firsts'.

'When the game's next chapter launched we set our alarm clocks for three in the morning, in order to wake up before school to play,' he says. 'Wanting to be the best, and wanting our guild to be *the first*. is what motivated me. It was exciting to reach an encounter and figure out how to beat it so you could say you were the first guys to do so. Not only were you praised for your speed by others, but you had the enjoyment of figuring out how to beat the challenge.'

Edmond was a keen sportsman and musician at school but the thrill of acquiring a world first in *World of Warcraft* offered, he says, a far greater buzz than 'beating another group of sixteen-year-old kids from a small town'. Edmond was an accomplished student. He was active in the science fair and regularly entered national school jazz band competitions. But something about competing on an international scale within *World of Warcraft* offered a greater thrill than anything he had yet experienced.

'I was into spreadsheets and mathematics, so I did a lot of the strategising for the group,' he says. 'I loved trying to find the optimal solution to a problem. I could use logic, math and problem-solving and I could find answers that would cause people all over the world to change the way in which they approached the game. To be admired by so many people was a great feeling. It started to get more serious once I took on more of a role in the guild. We were popular in this online world, and the power and attention was an amazing feeling for a sixteen-year-old kid from a small town.'

As Edmond's role in the guild developed and he developed leadership qualities, he found the way in which he interacted with others outside of the game began to subtly shift.

'It was hard for a shy kid like me to stand up and boss people around,' he says. 'As I started to develop this assertiveness it caused me some problems at school as I went from somebody people listened to and respected in the game world to just another kid in a sea of schoolchildren. At that age it was really hard to keep both worlds separate. It was easy to want to value the game world more than the real world as I felt more appreciated there.

Powergaming is the pursuit of the time-rich, the domain of students and the unemployed, those who are able to dedicate the swathes of time necessary to master the game and then maintain their mastery. But this approach to playing games also demands a certain type of player, the kind of human who can maintain focus on a single goal at the expense of all others. For Edmond, the dedication he gave reflects the part of his personality that wants to compete and to become the best.

For Boyle, however, the obsession reflects something that he views as a negative aspect to his personality.

'It was an absolute loss of time,' he says. 'I took nothing good away from it. Instead I lost several years of my life I could have done something else with. It was a cause of concern and disgust for my family, like a bad drug addiction where you would sacrifice nearly everything for the monthly subscription and internet access. Those days were far from glamorous, and what money was made from playing got dumped back into the games to fuel the addiction. It took boredom for me to finally break the cycle.'

While many powergamers set aside the pursuit of in-game excellence as they grow older and the demands of adulthood squeeze free time and energy, the inner mentality developed through these experiences is not so easily discarded.

'To this day I still enjoy playing games at the top tier,' says Edmond. 'When you're just a casual player you muddle through. When you're at the top level, you have to experiment and truly understand the concepts. This gives you more freedom in a way. Most of us still enjoy the challenge of figuring out a game and getting to the top, but we no longer desire the stagnant gameplay of remaining there.'

Today Boyle warns others away from this mode of play. But Edmond is more pragmatic.

'Don't listen to all those horror stories about people who ruined their lives this way,' he says. 'People ruin their lives with partying. People ruin their lives by trying to be professional athletes. You can find scare stories about people destroying their lives doing almost anything. Setting a goal and accomplishing it is one of the greatest things a person can do.'

For each of these players around the world, video games provided a clear and, crucially, achievable goal – one that came with the promise of peer approval and kudos. Whether you're being applauded for your performance on the *Dance Dance Revolution* machine, for your world-record-breaking high score in a thirty-year-old arcade game, or for your character's hard-won cloak in an online game, these video games provide an accessible route to glory. In reality, success is rarely reported so straightforwardly. Virtual attainment is an illusion we willingly serve, sometimes at the cost of genuine personal, professional, financial, social or spiritual progress and, more pertinently, as a dependable stand-in for when those things prove elusive. Video games give us a sense of achievement that is, in the moment at least, indistinguishable from success outside of the game.

And in the leaderboard, that semi-permanent record of a person's achievements, there is a kind of immortality, a reassurance that, contrary to what many might believe, this wasn't a waste of time, an endeavour that will be lost the moment the machine is switched off.

Video games record our achievements (the modern consoles even use the terminology, recording in-game achievements as part of an enduring player's profile that, presumably, they will carry throughout their lives). We talk of 'saving' our progress in a game, making a permanent record of what we've done within their reality. Video games are perhaps a kind of immortality project, a way to save the memory of our progress in life, a way to find glory through victory in competition and, ultimately, a way to somehow endure.

03

LOST IN THE SYSTEM

INSERT COIN TO CONTINUE

The man approaches the booth, his face a scrawl of worry lines, his eyes determined. He slides his papers across the desk.

'What is the purpose of your trip?' I ask.

'Today is a beautiful day, my friend,' he replies, ignoring the question with the amiable defiance of the octogenarian.

He and his wife have, he explains, fled the tyranny of their home country, Antegria. They have come to seek asylum, here in Arstotzka.

His story is affecting, but largely irrelevant. In *Papers, Please*, a video game set in a fictional (yet historically realistic) 1980s-era eastern European communist country, would-be immigrants are assaulting the border. Many are just as deserving of refuge as this man and his bent-backed wife, who shifts her weight between feet as she waits in line behind her husband.

My job as the immigration inspector at the Grestin Border Checkpoint is not to weigh the truth or worth of these stories. Rather, it is to check that each person's papers are in order and, ideally, to find them lacking and deny entry. It pays to make snap decisions: the more people I process in a day, the more money I take home to my family.

But the bureaucracy is chaotic: every day a fresh set of rules and checks is sent from the capital, new knots in the red tape designed to make access that much harder for the asylum seekers at the gates.

Mistakes are costly: my pay is docked for each person I let through in error. My wages do not cover the food, heating and medicine I need to feed, clothe and heal my family, so the more mistakes that are made, the starker my choices become. When there's a limited amount of money in the pot, you must decide which loved ones to care for. Who will spend today panged with sickness or hunger?

The man's papers are in order.

But as I stamp them he looks anything but relieved.

'*Please* be kind to my wife,' he says, shuffling off across no man's land with its mad dogs and swivelling searchlights. 'She is just after me.'

Moments later she approaches the window, slow with age and anxiety.

'Did you see my husband?' she asks. 'He made it through, yes?'

Her passport seems in order but when I ask to see her entry permit her face blanches.

'They would not give me permit,' she says. 'I have no choice. I will be killed if I return to Antegria. Please, I beg you.'

The difficult decisions have come earlier than usual today. My choice is plain: save the bureaucracy or save the marriage and, possibly, the life.

Our world is built upon invisible rules and systems.

The natural laws govern when the sun rises and falls. They specify the tug of gravity, the timing of the seasons, the gestation of a pregnancy, the direction in which rivers flow, the way flowers are pollinated, the need for water and for love.

Then there are the human-made laws and systems. They govern our behaviour, determining the side of the road on which all cars must drive and the speed limit that drivers must adhere to. There are systems in place for when these rules are broken.

There are rules that set the time at which street lights flicker to life and dictate whether or not a person is allowed to pass from one country to the next. They specify who is allowed healthcare, how many items we are allowed in our basket at the supermarket checkout and the amount of money and support that our state offers those in need.

We refer to the legal system, the school system, the healthcare system. We talk of broken systems, referring to when things don't work as they should. We say: 'the system works!' often with disbelief, when they do.

Our own bodies function thanks to thousands of interrelated systems, the complexities of the human organism with its wending blood, churning waste, fizzing oxygen, enzymes, antibodies, nerve endings and biorhythms. We exist not only within systems but *because of* systems, without which we could not live, breathe, walk, talk or think. Systems not only govern our lives, they also facilitate them.

It is not only logical but inevitable that our video games should be built from rules and systems that reflect those of our experience. These rules might be as basic as *Pong* (1972), the primitive tennis game (with its timeless and elegantly succinct instruction: 'avoid missing ball for high-score'), or they might be as complex as *Grand Theft Auto V* (2013), a game that attempts to recreate the American city of Los Angeles at both a geographical, environmental and socio-political level. But no matter how complex or straightforward, a video game is a microcosm, a virtual reality, a place governed by the sorts of rules and systems that human beings experience in their everyday lives. You might have to plan to visit the shops during opening hours in *Animal Crossing*, *Shenmue* or *Oblivion*, or learn to abide by a strict timetable in the *Densha de Go!* series

61

in which you play as a harangued Japanese subway train driver, racing to keep his train on time lest his pay be docked for running late.

In laying down the systems that govern their virtual world, video-game makers are omniscient creators with the power of a god. The creator usually starts with the natural laws. They set down the mountains and arrange the valleys in their world. The creator decides upon the sky's hue, the water's viscosity, the pitch of birdsong and the force of gravity's pull. The creator types 'let there be light' (or the programming equivalent) and there is light. The creator chooses how and when night falls and whether or not there will be a new dawn. The creator conjures how time works (linear, malleable or something else entirely) and writes the strands of code that form the incumbent creatures' DNA. Then, when everything is planned out, the creator clicks 'RUN' to execute a microcosmic Big Bang.

The author occupies a similar role when constructing the world in which their story will take place. They too set the rules of their fiction, lay the terrain and the architecture that rises from it, invent the people that will inhabit these landscapes and conjure the props that they use. Fiction is the sphere in which the human creator can taste this kind of divine creator power. But the video game is the only medium that forces an audience to experience first-hand the rules and systems by which the creator's fictional worlds operate.

Naturally, video games often attempt to distinguish themselves from the mundane texture and circumstance of everyday life by presenting us with the opportunity to enter situations (and systems) that are too dangerous or expensive for reality.

The earliest video games sent their players to dogfight in outer space (*Spacewar*, 1962) or to hurtle around a racetrack in a

Ferrari Testarossa (*Hard Drivin'*, 1989), exciting experiences that are either outside the realm of possibility or outside the reach of affordability for most people. More recent titles continue the theme. We assume the role of marines on the Middle Eastern front line (*Call of Duty*, 2003–), an international football star (*FIFA*, 1993–) or a cheap-suited member of the Japanese mafia (*Yakuza*, 2005–).

Increasingly, video-game creators have turned their focus from obviously perilous scenarios to less extreme yet, for most, equally alien places and systems in life. *SimCity* allows us to experience the stresses and pressures of being a city planner while, in *Oddworld: Abe's Oddysee*, we assume life as an alien slave worker born into captivity. In *Prison Architect* (2015) we are made responsible for both the architectural layout of an American prison and its day-to-day running, balancing the needs and human rights of our prisoners with the bottom line. *Smuggle Truck* (2011) casts you as the driver of a truck filled with would-be immigrants, trying to carry them across the border (Apple initially rejected the game from the App Store based on its controversial theme. When developer Owlchemy Labs changed the game's title to *Snuggle Truck*, and changed the immigrants to cuddly toys, the game was accepted onto the store).

In *Plague Inc.* (2012) we assume the role of a virus, attempting to survive, evolve and propagate till we have travelled to every country in the world and infected every living human. *Coming Out Simulator 2014* is a simple, autobiographical game about a young man's experiences trying to tell his parents about his sexual orientation. Where else but inside the dimensions of a video game could we experience the life of Dr Mohammed Mossadegh, the first democratically elected prime minister of Iran's, pet cat (*The Cat and the Coup*, 2011)?

Many video games present not only the natural and legal or

municipal rules and systems of the world, but also the social ones. *Persona 4* (2008) recreates the pressures and perils of growing up in high school, with its cliques and disorientating group dynamics (even though the game is set in a Japanese high school, the idiosyncrasies of the country's education system are less important than the universal themes of adolescence). *Coolest Girl in School* (2007) presents its player with the dilemma of how to make it through the day if you end up with a period stain on your skirt (a common, unifying experience for women that's almost never mentioned in entertainment).

Like *Papers, Please, Cart Life* is another affecting video-game study of life inside a broken system, this time of contemporary life in America for those working on the poverty line. The game follows the lives of recent immigrants as they attempt to earn a living as street vendors. Andrus, for example, sells newspapers to make the rent. Melanie runs a coffee stand in the hope doing so will prove to the authorities she is responsible enough to look after her daughter.

Just as you feel something of a chemical cocktail of fear and excitement as you breach the back door of a terrorist hideout in *Call of Duty*, so *Cart Life* elicits honest empathy with its protagonists through its systems. As you experience something of their lives you begin to feel the pain of systemic unfairness and economic failure first-hand. The pain of inequality is theirs but, as you assume their roles, it's also somehow yours – at least till the video game is switched off and the unreality pricked. The sense of injustice when Andrus is evicted from his motel room for keeping a cat, his only friend and companion, is devastating.

So too is the elderly woman's plain statement back at the Arstotzka checkpoint in *Papers, Please* as you turn her away for being unable to produce the necessary permit.

'You have doomed me,' she says, as she walks away, unable to join her husband.

One of the earliest games I played as a child was *Missile Command*. The game was different to the others on the compendium my grandmother bought for me on my twelfth birthday, even if there was nothing to distinguish its stark and basic graphics from the rest. Your task in the game isn't to assume the role of an all-powerful military commander. Rather, you're cast in the role of a regional commander charged with protecting six cities from a nuclear rain of ICBMs. As the enemy nukes streak through a black sky towards your cities, you fire rockets that, if well aimed, will blast the incoming danger from the sky, thereby protecting the citizens under your protection.

For all the game's apparent simplicity (there are no reams of explanatory text, no characters to give voice to the unfolding horror), it had a terrible power, something that I could sense as a child, even if I couldn't grasp its full subtleties. Where does this power originate? *Missile Command* is a non-violent game: you don't launch any attacks on your unknown, unseen enemy. Your task is merely to save cities and the lives within. It's not a game that glorifies military might; it focuses on the experience of being on the receiving end of a nuclear strike.

As you play through *Missile Command*, a story riddled with moral consequence unfolds. You only have a limited supply of rockets and, as such, you are soon presented with awful choices: do you try to spread your limited resources across your cities, risking failure but knowing that you tried to save everyone equally? Or do you focus on just one location that you can more ably defend, but at the cost of seeing the others burn to the ground (after all, you lose the game only when all six cities are destroyed)? Do you defend your missile silos, prioritising military lives over civilians? Or do you allow your dutiful soldiers, who have been carrying out your orders unquestioningly, to die? Even as a child I understood something of the horror of the moment-to-moment choices with which I was being presented, and felt something of the dread and stress that any commander in a similar position would surely endure.

Perhaps most terribly, no matter how many stages you survive, there is no way to win the game. As in most games of the time, failure is inevitable. In the end, everyone dies. And yet here, in this context, failure seemed to carry more weight.

Missile Command, first designed in 1980, is an early example of a video game that combines system and theme to provide commentary on the world. The power of play within systems here is apparent. In an interview, given years after *Missile Command*'s release, the game's creator, Dave Theurer, said:

'I'd wake up in the middle of the night from a nightmare where I'd see these streaks coming in, and I'd be up in the Santa Cruz mountains and I'd see it hit Sunnyvale and I'd know I had about 45 seconds until the blast reached me. I had those nightmares once a month for a year after I finished *Missile Command*.'

Whether or not a game comes to haunt your dreams, the combination of its system and chosen theme almost always results in some kind of statement, either explicit or implicit. Sometimes the system is enough to speak to us: *Snakes and Ladders* is a simple game about life's capriciousness. At other times the system must be paired with a fiction for it to become meaningful: *Risk* is a game about imperialism and the expansion of dominion, and the ensuing complications as you protect that territory. Likewise, *Monopoly* is a game about capitalism: it encourages its players to acquire real estate with the dog-eat-dog competitiveness of the international marketplace (we begin the game all smiles and carefree ambition, and end it either grimly destroyed or monstrously victorious).

The same is true of many video games, which cannot help but cast light on our world as they borrow rules, systems and scenarios from reality. Even those video games that appear to share few similarities with our existence are often built upon familiar systems that can, occasionally, reveal some truth about the world in which we live or, at very least, allow us to examine the world and its rules in a manageable context. *Tetris*, you might argue, is a game that replicates the sense of being overwhelmed as life's problems and demands pile up more quickly than you are able to clear them away. Most adventure and role-playing games mimic the same consumerist loops of acquisition, as you are made to feel constantly dissatisfied with your equipment and possessions each time you reach a new shop and find a slightly better sword or cloak. *Journey* is a game in which players drift into and out of each other's experiences trudging through a desert, able to share a moment together but not any kind of virtual touch (you cannot communicate or share names), and quietly speaks to the essential inscrutability and existential impossibility of human relationships.

Video games offer a cat's cradle of interlocking systems, often based on those found in reality, for a player to wrestle and reckon with. And here we find something of their enduring appeal and irresistible draw, the kind of draw that inspires some to almost fully emigrate from real life to virtual. Just as humans attempt to make sense of the world around them, to find their own place within the systems both natural and human-made that control the ebb and flow of existence, so video games encourage us to wrestle with life and our place in the world. They are a manageable, safe and usually reliable environment in which to play with ideas about our existence or the systems in which we live.

But there's something else, too. A game's reality is underpinned not by the unpredictability of our world, where people who work the hardest do not necessarily triumph; most games treat the player with unflinching justice (when they don't, it's usually classed as a bug). The game makes its player a fair bargain: 'Give me your time and energy and you will prevail in accordance with your effort.' It says: 'Work hard and victory will be yours. You will be glorious.'

And arguably no video game has allowed more people to reach for glory than *Minecraft*.

Among the medium's pantheon of gurus, rock stars and auteurs, Markus Persson, the Swedish creator of *Minecraft* – a video game that has, in the few years since its initial release, become a twenty-first-century sensation, played in bedrooms and classrooms around the world – is something of a Zeus. More than twenty-five million people have paid to immigrate to his world and settle there, be it on PC, smartphone or video-game console. Released without backing from investors or publishers, *Minecraft* is inspiring a new generation of independent game makers to strike out on their own, and to approach their medium in new ways. Meanwhile, the profits it's generated – $128 million in 2013, the year before Microsoft bought Persson's company, Mojang, for $2.5 billion – rival those of the world's largest entertainment releases.

Such incomparable success is unexpected when you consider the game itself. *Minecraft* embodies few video-game fashions. It features pixellated scenery that has nothing in common with the lifelike, polygon-stuffed characters and objects that furnish the blockbuster video games of the day. There is a certain Lego-like charm and blunt handsomeness to the rectangular clouds that throw shadows over the game's pea-green hills. But in an industry traditionally obsessed with chasing photorealism, its kindergarten aesthetic at first appears anachronistic.

Released long before it was finished, *Minecraft* has no in-game tutorial, no instruction pages and few explicit goals. The basic rules are inscrutable, and, for players brought up on to-do list play, the passage of time largely aimless. And yet, in a few short months, *Minecraft* made Persson, who is known to many of his millions of fans by his nickname 'Notch', a multimillionaire, and revealed its audience to be one of the most creatively motivated in video games.

Why? Perhaps it's the comfort of experiencing an intelligent design that reveals a watchmaker's precision. Or maybe the elemental freedom that *Minecraft* offers its inhabitants taps into some primal, irresistible human urge to build. Undoubtedly, here is a game that offers an accelerated form of existence – of dominion but also of stewardship. The in-game story of *Minecraft* is the story of humankind: survival, hunting, community and, eventually, hubris. It is a video game that allows us to wrestle with humanity's common question: what are we here for?

The story goes like this: in the beginning you're given your own algorithmically generated world (each new game creates an expanse of blocky geology that nobody, not even Persson, has seen before). Day one and your goal is mere exploration. You chart the terrain around you, a carefree sort of cartography as you feel out the contours of your domain, marvel at the scenery and build a mental map of natural landmarks by which to set your bearings.

Other than this there is little more than the game's instructive title to provide a clue to your task: to mine and to craft. These twin abilities – destruction and creation – are mapped to the game's two main buttons. Press one and your stumpy arm will flail in front of you with comic speed and repetition, chipping away at whatever object you're looking at, eventually reducing it to a floating cube of material that may be collected and stored in your inventory. The nature of the harvest is dependent on the material you 'mine'. Chop a tree and you will produce a block of wood. A cliff face will yield a chunk of granite. Hammer the beach and you'll nab a cube of sand. With these raw materials you are free to build.

At first you might experiment with a waist-high wall, laying blocks side by side in a straight line. Now, emboldened by your success, you turn it into one of the four walls of a small house, blocking out the light with a flat roof before knocking through the door you neglected to account for in the original design.

Meanwhile, the sun has wheeled in the sky, its plodding arc unnoticed by the novice (*Minecraft* imitates our world's day/night cycle, albeit in an accelerated form). Night falls and the eerie sounds of scratching monsters arise. These are the game's dead-eyed zombies, its clinking skeletons and camouflaged creepers (a kind of weaponised hedge), whose kindergarten path-finding AI has them pursue you with nightmarish single-mindedness. At this point *Minecraft*'s ambiance shifts, and you realise that while this world is a playpen for the imagination, it is also a place of peril.

In a flash you switch from tourist to tormented. Your goal shifts to a quest for survival. You retreat into your creation or, if it remains unfinished, hurriedly hollow out a cave in the side of a mountain in which to quiver and cringe till morning, when the skeletons and zombies dissipate like Dracula in sunlight and you're free to return to your construction.

This is the side of *Minecraft* that mimics the natural order: the ever-present danger of being eaten by something that is larger or stronger than ourselves, the need to find shelter to hide from this threat.

Survive the night and the next day you continue with the implementation of your half-cocked ideas. The hut becomes a shack becomes a lodge becomes a house becomes a mansion becomes a castle. You soon learn that certain blocks require certain tools, and using a craft bench you begin to fashion simple utensils: a pickaxe, a shovel, a hoe, a sword. As the range of blocks you've harvested diversifies so the range of domestic features you can build widens. Soon your abode is furnished with candles, paintings, elaborate stairwells and bay windows.

The pleasure of construction is matched by the thrill of destruction, our play reflecting the very rhythms of life: birth, death and rebirth. *Minecraft* understands that, for humans, the business of creation is closely linked to the business of survival. The threat of the monsters that click and ramble in the dark brings focus to your industry, while the richness of materials found in the world facilitates the personal touch, encouraging craftsmanship.

Minecraft is a game that enables humans to experience an accelerated or distilled form of human life. Behind the lumpy pixels – the crude trees, the jagged mountains, the simple sun – lies a game about the systems of existence. In a post-industrialised world, it's also (curiously enough for a game played on the latest technological devices) a game about returning to nature, to the basics of survival and perseverance.

We play *Minecraft* in our millions as a way to understand our most ancient purposes in the universe: to survive and to create. In its straightforward distillation of our world's fundamental rules and systems, we are able to better understand who we are and why we build.

These twin urges can be found in most video games. In 1984's *Elite* we travel through a primitive galaxy, fending off attacks from aliens while attempting to build a business as a mineral trader. In 1989's *SimCity* we have the opportunity to build a city from the ground up, carefully placing streets, homes and industrial factories, while attempting to survive the ravages of an unexpected earthquake. In 2008's *LittleBigPlanet* we create intricate Super Mario-style levels, built from a mess of ropes, pulleys, toilet rolls, fruit, footballs and skateboards, and then attempt to guide our character, Sackboy, towards their conclusion without catching fire, or tripping off a ledge to his death.

These games, alongside *Minecraft*, demonstrate clearly the ways in which video games give a person the opportunity to survive and thrive within a system. But when more than one human being enters a multifaceted video-game system, another of those primal urges surfaces: the desire to cooperate with others, to work in community.

Minecraft itself allows for this kind of collaboration. Special servers allow players from around the world to play alongside one another inside a shared world, working on large-scale projects of their own making. Cooperation in *Minecraft* is straightforward: people come together and build things. There is not much need for governance. But *Minecraft* is a relatively simple proposition. Other multiplayer video games are built from more complex systems and allow different sorts of human expression, collaboration and rivalry. These realities require something a little more formalised, something closer to the councils, governments and groups that administer the systems we find in our own reality. And in these games we see not only echoes of the natural world in which we live, but also the social and political systems in which we operate.

Launched in 2003, *EVE Online* is a science-fiction video game of unprecedented scale and ambition, a cosmos comprising 7,500 interconnected star systems and home to more than half a million people who barter, fight and collaborate with one another in what has become a vast and fascinating social experiment.

As in life, your experience in the game is largely dictated by where you are born and live. High Security dwellers can keep a low profile as they eke out an honest living as a miner or trader, earning money with which to improve their ship or dwelling. The Null Spacers, who live in the galactic equivalent of the Wild West, by contrast, throw themselves into a Machiavellian world of intrigue, engaging in dynamic, player-led plotlines, conspiracies and intergalactic heists.

In one notorious incident a few years ago, members of a mercenary group worked for twelve months to infiltrate a powerful in-game corporation. They took on jobs within the company's structure and ingratiated themselves with its staff. Then, in one orchestrated attack, the group seized the company's assets, ambushed its female CEO, blew up her ship and delivered her frozen corpse to the client who paid for the assassination. Not only was this an act of astounding coordination but it had real-world value too: the virtual assets seized were worth tens of thousands of US dollars.

Few video games accommodate the unpredictability of human interaction and will with such freedom. For that reason, *EVE*'s population is diverse and enthusiastic. But for its developer, CCP Games, this presents a significant problem. How to develop and evolve the galaxy in such a way that it keeps everyone, from the day-tripping explorer to the money-grubbing space pirate, content. The solution? The Council of Stellar Management (CSM), a democratically elected player council whose job is to represent the interests of the game's vast population to its Icelandic creators.

Each year scores of would-be player–politicians stand for the CSM. Just fourteen of those who campaign are elected. Every six months CCP flies the successful candidates to their headquarters in Reykjavik for three days of intensive debate. During that time the council meets with CCP's in-house economist, Dr Eyjólfur Guðmundsson, and hears about the new features planned for the galaxy's future. If necessary, they can contest these proposals in the interests of their electorate. Minutes are kept of each meeting and made public afterwards, so there's full transparency as to whether a councillor is making good on their campaign promises.

'Council members can have very different ambitions and concerns depending on which part of space they hail from,' explains CCP's Ned Coker. 'You may have somebody who lives in the galaxy's outer reaches and, as such, they will have a very different viewpoint to those that live in a more centralised area.' Likewise, would-be councillors often campaign on specific issues, promising that, should they be elected, they'll ensure they promote the interests of those who voted for them.

The run-up to the annual election reflects the way in which political parties work in real life.

'Candidates come with their own platforms, create propaganda and do a lot of mustering both in the game and out in order to get elected,' says Coker. This year David Whitelaw, an oil-rig worker from the small town of Thurso on the north coast of Scotland, decided to attempt to interview every candidate in the final ballot for his *EVE*-themed podcast.

'Candidates loosely fall within three categories,' he says. 'There are those who stand on a single issue. Then others who champion a specific play style such as piracy or industry or who represent a large group of alliances. Finally, there are those who propose to act purely as a communication membrane between CCP and the players. Lesser-known players will have to put more hours into campaigning than prominent candidates and even then they are at a huge disadvantage. Having a positive profile in the community is a huge advantage.'

In May 2013, after months of campaigning both within the game and across social media, the line-up of the eighth CSM was announced. It's the fifth time that fifty-four-year-old Robert Woodhead from Wilmington, North Carolina, has been elected as a council member. A seasoned veteran, these days Woodhead campaigns on his favourable track record, although his experience doesn't preclude some grassroots leafleting. Last year he harvested thousands of player names from the game's web forums and sent an in-game email to each, encouraging them to 'Get out to vote' when the polls opened.

'I view the elections as good clean political fun, even a part of the actual game experience,' he says. 'You are being elected to be an advocate, not a legislator, and the campaign lets you demonstrate how well you can advocate.' That advocacy is, according to Woodhead, surprisingly effective.

'I have watched the CSM evolve over the past few years into a very useful tool for influencing the company,' he says. 'More and more people at CCP have come to realise that our feedback and advice is tremendously valuable, and we do help shape the game.'

CCP's Coker agrees. 'As a business we always get final say when it comes to whether or not we choose to act on the CSM's lobbying,' he says. 'But it behoves us to listen to the council. They are a distillation of the game's populace and they also hold a pretty large sway through their reputations. We've seen individuals in the council make extreme efforts to impress upon people that they are standing up to the "man" if we make an unpopular decision in terms of game design or development. To some degree they have been successful.'

Indeed, in 2011 CCP held an emergency meeting with the CSM following in-game riots after the developer decided to take a more aggressive approach to selling virtual items. Disgruntled players believed that the introduction of micro-transactions – which offered items of virtual clothing, accessories and mementoes for real money (including, for example, a $70 monocle) – was evidence that the game was moving in an unwelcome direction.

'The riots happened because CCP prioritised their vision over the needs of their customers,' explains Woodhead. 'They lost sight of the fundamental reason for *EVE*'s success – the depth and complexity of the social relationships that it spawns.'

The emergency summit demonstrated CCP's commitment to listening to their players and showed that the CSM has real power in representing the views of the game's populace.

'Some people think the CSM is a PR stunt,' says Coker. 'There are always conspiracy theorists. They think we flew them over here, got them drunk and told them what to say. But that incident showed the system works. Players not only felt like the CSM was working hard for them (after all, they all put their real jobs and lives on hold for a week), but also they held us to task.'

While the CSM is closer to a lobbying group than a governing body, it's not immune to corruption. Councillors are privy to forthcoming changes in the game and some unscrupulous members have used this information to their advantage. In 2009 one councillor, Adam Ridgway, bought items worth thousands of pounds for stockpiling ahead of a game-design change that would drastically increase their value. As these virtual items carry significant real-world worth, CCP closely monitors the actions of both CSM members and its own internal staff who play the game.

'We hold the CSM to a high standard,' says Coker. 'We even have an internal affairs department that follows players to see they're not using insider information for personal gain.' Ridgway stepped down from his position on the CSM as a result of his indiscretion.

Sociologists and economists increasingly study *EVE Online*. 'Within Eve we can see a political community that models hierarchy, authority, rule of law, power, violence and distribution of labour,' says Felix Ciuta, senior lecturer in international politics at UCL. Players project onto this blank space their political and ideological principles. The way in which people act in the game might not reflect the way in which they act in the real world. But their virtual behaviour almost certainly is an expression of their ideas about how the world really works. Its populace is, when set against the Western world's increasingly disaffected electorate, energised and politically engaged. Why? Perhaps its players find here a virtual world that they are able to affect in meaningful ways, where their voice and actions are heard and seen. The game makes visible and comprehensible a political system that, in life, is often opaque, confusing and, to some, distant. Even in the farthest reaches of virtual outer space the game reflects our world and, for some, makes it more approachable.

Birth, life, creation, hubris, death and politics: at least some of the appeal of these video-game realities is that they offer a means to understand the world around us, in manageable chunks.

They are usually built upon familiar and recognisable rules and systems. The recognition evolves into comfort when it's possible for us to triumph within those systems: they imply that our world, too, is fair, when in fact it is, very often, capricious and unfair. Witness how game designers try to turn the slippery and mysterious act of falling in love into a manageable, reliable system (often to ridiculous effect). In *The Sims* you can make someone fall in love with you by tickling them repeatedly; in *Harvest Moon* you make someone fall in love with you by presenting them with an egg laid by one of your chickens each day; in *Fire Emblem*, relationships are formed through mere proximity to others on a battlefield.

Moreover, video games flatter us: their worlds exist for our benefit, and, usually, revolve around us. A video game requires a player: without input, it is inert. Our world, by contrast, seems indifferent to us. The cogs around us, both natural and human-made, turn regardless of our interest or input. It is sometimes difficult to know whether we matter, whether anyone cares. When a company loses our details or forgets about us for some reason, we talk of being 'lost in the system'. This is how loneliness is seeded in the human heart: a sense that the world and all of its people are indifferent, oblivious.

Video games are different. They deal in the language of cause and effect; they offer constant feedback to our interactions. Their sound effects offer an aural indication that our presence and interest have been registered. Their high-score tables offer encouragement as well as the hope of improvement and yet further approval.

Likewise, a video game's creator is not a distant, seemingly uninvolved god. He, she or they not only lay down the rules of the creation's existence; they are also on hand to listen to our comments and cries, the feedback that many then use to iterate and improve upon virtual existence. Often, in video games, there is a back and forth between a creator and the people who live within his or her creation. In these realities, we have an opportunity to influence the systems that govern us.

Marilynn Strasser Olson, in her 1991 biography of the American illustrator and writer Ellen Raskin, wrote, 'Games as arbiters of rules and objectives are a metaphor for a vision of life that can be ordered, understood, and won.' We play video games in order to be comforted by a particular vision of life, an ordering at times dramatic and at times systemic. In this way they share an essential characteristic with literature: the fiction brings order and sense to the randomness of life. Video games comfort us as their worlds abide by certain rules and order. Moreover, they present us with the opportunity to master the rules and to flourish. It's something that goes beyond mere victories of plot, in which we rescue the prince or princess, vanquish the antagonist, save the world. It's in the way in which our video-game characters visibly overcome obstacles and trials, their progress measured in distance travelled, or points gained.

Like sport, video games make simple the criteria for success and failure. They clearly establish their rules and parameters, and explain what we must do in order to progress. Their screens are less like windows to other worlds and more like mirrors that reflect how our world functions.

Superficially, at least, video games improve upon some aspects of our own reality. For a human who has experienced life's petty and major injustices, what better place is there to spend one's time than in a virtual world, where struggle always leads to success, where effort is repaid in kind, where there is justice and glory for any and all who want it? In their ordered systems, we catch a glimpse of a kind of prevailing justice, which our own world is often unable to match.

04

DISCOVERY

On 28 March 2011, a man who calls himself Kurt J. Mac loaded a new game of *Minecraft*. As the landscape filled in around his character, Mac surveyed the blocky, pixellated trees, the cloud-draped mountains, and the waddling sheep. Then he started walking. His goal for the day was simple: to reach the end of the universe.

Nearly three years later, Mac, who is now thirty-one, is still walking. He has trekked more than seven hundred virtual kilometres in a hundred and eighty hours. At his current pace, Mac will not reach the edge of the world, which is now nearly twelve thousand kilometres away, for another twenty-two years.

In the four years since its initial release, *Minecraft* has become a phenomenon that is played by more than forty million people around the world, on computers, smartphones and video-game consoles. It is primarily a game about human expression: a giant, Lego-style construction set in which every object can be broken down into its constituent elements and rebuilt in the shape of a house, an airship, a skyscraper or whatever else a player can create.

Minecraft's universe is procedurally generated, meaning that an algorithm places each asset – every hill, mountain, cave, river, sheep, and so on – in a unique arrangement every time a new game is loaded, so that no two players' worlds are exactly alike. Markus Persson, the game's creator, planned for these worlds to be infinitely large: if a player kept walking in a single direction, the game would create more of the world in front of him, like an engineer forever laying track for an advancing train.

But, at extreme distances from a player's starting point, a glitch in the underlying mathematics causes the landscape to fracture into illogical shapes and patterns.

'Pretty early on, when implementing the "infinite" worlds, I knew the game would start to bug out at long distances,' Persson told me. 'But I did the math on how likely it was people would ever reach it, and I decided it was far away enough that the bugs didn't matter.'

In March 2011, Persson wrote a blog post about the problem in the game's source code and the mysterious area where *Minecraft's* world begins to warp and disintegrate, a place that he calls the Far Lands. Around that time, inspired by the legions of *Minecraft* players who record and broadcast their adventures, Mac started a YouTube channel to document his virtual exploits. As he cast about for a fresh angle to distinguish his episodes from those of other YouTube *Minecraft*-casters, he came upon Persson's post. It was exactly what Mac had been searching for: he changed the name of his YouTube channel to Far Lands or Bust!, and he set off to see them for himself.

'In my ignorance, I thought the journey might take a year or so,' Mac tells me. 'Had I known that the Far Lands were so many thousands of kilometres away, I might have been more hesitant.'

In his essential book about video games, *Trigger Happy*, the writer and critic Steven Poole argues, 'The jewel in the crown of what video games can offer is the aesthetic emotion of wonder.' This is achieved most readily, he writes, via the awe-inspiring places and scenes that video-game designers build on our screens, 'cathedrals of fire', in his memorable phrase.

Few who have, for example, stepped blinking from the murk and grime of *Oblivion*'s city sewers into the virtual kingdom of

Cyrodil's brilliant white sunlight would disagree with Poole's assertion. Here, miles of verdant countryside blanket out from your feet; hills, valleys and mountains that stretch away into the distance, inviting not only exploration, but also wonder.

There's a unique sense of awe to being a tourist in a place that's simultaneously vivid and virtual. It's a feeling that video games elicit with wonderful regularity. It's there when you crest a hill on horseback in *The Legend of Zelda: Ocarina of Time* while the sun sets and windmills wheel in the distance; it's there as you climb one of the stratospheric stone giants in *Shadow of the Colossus*, as you haul yourself upwards by grasping fistfuls of the moss that grows on its back; it's there in the sand-buffed structures found within the desert scenes of Sony's appropriately named *Journey*, objects that provide touch-points of humanity in an otherwise arid and forsaken desert. Video-game designers often seek to propel us through their worlds, laying down a crumb trail of objectives designed to hold our attention. But sometimes, the worlds they create cause us to put down the to-do list, to stop and stare at this forest, that horizon, those fields, these spaceships.

Video games allow us to enter into the roles and vocations of people unlike us; likewise, they enable us to visit and explore places that would be unreachable any other way. In their bounds we are able to satisfy the fidgety human desire to explore, to seek out the new and, ultimately perhaps, to call the new our own.

Their appeal is to be found in time, the way we can lose ourselves in the tasks they set before us, the rhythms of their interactions and rewards that lead to chronoslip. But it's also to be found in the spaces that they make available to us, the openings they provide into new planes of landscape and reality.

The honest sense of success that accompanies an achieved goal is crucial to the video game's appeal. But so too is the journey. In 1881 Robert Louis Stevenson articulated the idea in his book

Virginibus Puerisque, writing that 'to travel hopefully is a better thing than to arrive, and the true success is to labour'.

Stevenson, who two years later would publish his travelogue drama *Treasure Island,* would find the maxim borne out in fiction as well as life – as too do we video-game explorers, questing hopefully through virtual domains more than a century later.

In contrast to Columbus, Drake, Dampier and all the other drivers of the age of discovery, with their bulging galleons full of supplies, Mac prepared for his hike through *Minecraft* in only a basic way. He gathered the materials to craft a sword, for protection, and a pickaxe, for digging rudimentary shelters to hide from the game's lethal nocturnal terrors.

'Most important, I brought a compass,' he says. 'The compass always points toward the original spawn point. That way, I would know that, as long as I walk in the direction opposite the needle's point, I am headed in the right direction.'

Mac has filmed his entire odyssey, breaking it up into separate YouTube episodes, across multiple seasons.

'The YouTube format serves the journey well, allowing the viewer to experience the entire adventure along with me,' he says. 'Also, if anyone had doubts as to whether or not I was making this trek to the Far Lands without cheating, they could go back and watch all of the footage.'

But Mac soon realised that he would have to fill each episode with commentary, both to engage his audience and to stave off loneliness.

'The series transformed into a sort of podcast, where the topics I talk about might have little to do with the journey itself,' he says. 'Of course, it is always exciting when *Minecraft* regrabs my attention with a perilous cliff, a zombie attack, or a memorable landscape, and I remember the journey I'm on.'

By one measure, Mac's endeavour is motivated by the same spirit that propels any explorer towards the far reaches of the unknown. Today, we live in a world meticulously mapped by satellites and Google cars, making uncharted virtual lands some of the last places that can satisfy a yearning for the beyond, as well as locations where you are simply, as Mac puts it, 'first'.

'My viewers and I are the only people to ever see these places exactly as they are,' he says. 'Once we walk past, we will never see them again.'

While the premise of walking in a single direction through a video game for hundreds of hours may seem banal, *Minecraft* has a special ability to create unscripted character drama. In almost every one of Far Lands or Bust's three hundred or so episodes, each of which lasts for around thirty-five minutes, Mac encounters something of note.

'On 6 June 2011, in episode thirty-two, I tamed a wolf,' he recalls. 'He quickly became a fan favourite and my only companion on the trip. Unfortunately, on the final day of the season, Wolfie, as I'd named him, mysteriously disappeared during a break.'

Mac presumed that Wolfie had been glitched out of the game, and his disappearance lent a sour note to the season finale. But, in an unlikely plot twist, Mac was reunited with Wolfie during the first episode of season four, and the pair continued the journey together.

When Mac began his quest, he was employed as a web designer, but, as his channel attracted more viewers, he started generating enough advertising revenue to quit his job and make virtual exploration his sole career. In a way, his viewers have become his patrons, funding his trip in exchange for reports and updates, which are interesting enough to elicit their continued support.

The channel's success – today, it has more than three hundred thousand subscribers – has been such that Kurt adopted the pseudonym Mac to conceal his identity from fans who might try to locate his house, in the Chicago suburbs.

Persson is an avid supporter of the Far Lands journey.

'It was one of those things that kind of slowly crept into my awareness,' he told me. 'I heard about it from various places and eventually got around to watching an episode.'

Mac met Persson in Paris, in 2012, at the game's annual conference, where the pair shook hands.

'I think, despite no longer being involved in *Minecraft*'s development, Notch is very amused at the various ways people have chosen to play his game,' Mac says.

Persson watches Mac's videos while working. 'I find it strangely calming and Zen-like,' he said. 'It makes for an excellent background to programming. It's not something I would ever attempt myself, though. I don't think I have that kind of personality.'

In June 2011, Mac partnered with the charity Child's Play, which aims to improve the lives of hospitalised children by providing toys and games to more than seventy hospitals worldwide.

'The viewers have always motivated me with their generosity,' he says. 'It has allowed the series to become more than just about reaching the Far Lands in a video game, but actually making a difference in the real world.'

The charitable cause also gave Mac a reason to withhold how far he has travelled, in order to maintain a sense of mystery.

'I now only ever press F3 to display my coordinates when certain fund-raising goals have been met.' When the first fund-raising goal, $8,200 dollars, was met, on 14 November 2011, Mac discovered he had travelled more than two hundred and ninety-two thousand metres.

'After the next goal, twenty-nine thousand two hundred and twenty dollars, was met, on 12 August 2012, I pressed F3, to find I had travelled six hundred and ninety-nine thousand four hundred and ninety-two metres,' he says.

The date and time of Mac's arrival in the Far Lands is much debated. It's agreed that in a completely flat *Minecraft* world it would take a player 820 hours of continuous walking to reach the edge of the universe. But Mac is playing in a world that's interrupted by mountains, oceans and other obstacles, all of which affect the pace of his travel. And he often stops to admire his surroundings.

'Some say it will take more than three thousand episodes to reach my destination at my current rate,' he says. 'But I never really take the time to think about it myself. My mantra has always been that this is about the journey and not the destination.'

Nevertheless, Mac is already beginning to see clues that he is on course.

'I've started to experience some of the effects of travelling so far from spawn,' he says. 'Items and entities are somewhat disjointed from the terrain around them, causing a jitter as I walk.'

Some people expect these problems to increase as Mac walks farther from his starting point, and some think that the game will be unplayable long before he reaches the Far Lands. Mac is philosophical.

'We will see when we get there,' he says.

This urge for players to explore the extremities of existence has been a part of video games since the very beginning.

In 1961, members of MIT's Tech Model Railroad Club created *Spacewar*, one of the first video games that ran on the university's hulking $120,000 PDP-1 mainframe computer. *Spacewar*, like so many of the video games that would follow, took place in the cosmos. The setting was, in part, a practical decision: it was far easier for the earliest computers to render the blank canvas of space than the comparable complexities of rocks, hills or cities. But, for games like *Space Invaders*, *Asteroids* and *Defender*, there's more to the choice of space as a backdrop than utilitarian function. Space has always fascinated storytellers, and with the birth of the video game, humans finally discovered a way to explore its farthest reaches from the crunchy comfort of terra firma.

Early video games kept the stories simple, but it wasn't long before these representations of space offered more than merely a place to defend humanity from an alien threat. Through video-game simulations, which have become ever more sophisticated with technology's advance, we've had the opportunity to visit the otherwise unreachable and, increasingly, to discover truths about our own galaxy.

One of the first truly ambitious simulations of space was *Elite*, a spaceship game created in 1984 by two university undergraduates, one aged nineteen, the other twenty, working out of a cramped dormitory in Jesus College, Cambridge. In the game, players tour the universe in a dog-fighting mining vessel; the program employed vector mathematics to create vast swathes of space, filled with line-art asteroids and spacecraft, which tilted and spun as if their blueprints had popped into three-dimensional life. Every time the game loaded, there was a digital equivalent of the Big Bang: unimaginable vastness was created from almost nothing.

'In the early 1980s, a typical home computer would have just thirty-two kilobytes of memory – less than a typical e-mail today,' David Braben, the programmer who created the game with Ian Bell, tells me. Rather than manually plot star systems by typing the coordinates of stars and planets into a database, Braben tried using randomly generated numbers. This method reduced the amount of designer time required to birth a universe, but at a cost: every time the game was loaded, its suns, moons, planets and stars would be in a new arrangement. To overcome the randomness problem, Braben used the Fibonacci sequence as a seed from which identical galaxies would be generated each time the game was played, all within a computer program a fraction of the size of a photograph taken with a mobile phone today.

More recently, Braben has returned to the game of his youth for a sequel, *Elite: Dangerous*. This time, he used astronomy rather than the Fibonacci sequence to arrange his galaxy.

'I wanted to make the galaxy as accurate as possible so that the results of that exploration would make sense to people,' Braben says. 'In the game, every single star in the real night sky is present, some hundred and fifty thousand of them, and you can visit each one. Even the clouds of stars that make up the Milky Way are included: some four hundred billion stars, their planetary systems, and moons are present, all waiting to be explored.'

Whereas Kurt J. Mac chose to walk to the edge of *Minecraft* in order to discover things that no other eye has yet seen, in *Elite: Dangerous* the appeal for players is to be able to reach the stars that frame nightlife on earth. Indeed, the positions of the stars in the game have been drawn from the numerous publicly available sky surveys, which Braben and his team at Frontier, the Cambridge-based game developer, collated and merged. They used procedural models based on physics to fill in gaps where data was missing or incomplete.

'As you move farther from earth, the data becomes increasingly sketchy, but the galaxy still runs by the same rules,' Braben says. 'The hundred and fifty thousand star systems are taken from real-world data. But once you move beyond a few hundred light years we can only see the very brightest stars individually, so we use procedural techniques to augment the data.'

In Braben's eagerness to replicate not only the vastness and wonder of space, but also its accurate layout and structure for us to explore, we can see something of the power that video games have to democratise exploration, tourism and, even, space travel. No matter who you are, or where you live, if you have access to a computer and the means to buy the video game, you can visit previously unimaginably distant places from the comfort of your home or internet café. The draw is obvious.

But, in *Elite*'s case at least, Braben has found another secondary benefit to his work, a different kind of discovery altogether: the computer simulations have begun to expose flaws in our scientific understanding of the universe.

Floor van Leeuwen helps run the Gaia satellite project, which aims to chart a three-dimensional map of the Milky Way, at the Cambridge Institute of Astronomy. According to Van Leeuwen, models of space such as those seen in *Elite: Dangerous* are crucial to expanding our understanding of the universe.

'Computer simulations have played a very important role in astronomy for many decades,' he said. 'The kind of problems encountered in astrophysics are almost always well outside what can be represented through simple clean equations.'

Models are created by taking data gathered by recent space missions and using this to improve and test simulations such as that found in *Elite: Dangerous*. Van Leeuwen believes that it's in the disparity between real-world observations and computer simulations that advances are most readily made.

'Astronomy is a field where you find a continuous exchange between new observations and modelling,' he says. 'The conflicts that show up are generally due to simplifications made in the models, for which new observations can provide improved guidelines. There's a continuously evolving and developing understanding of space, in which both models and observations play important roles.'

Elite: Dangerous has thrown up a number of conflicts between its model of the Milky Way and previous astronomical assumptions.

'Our night sky is based on real data – it is not a hand-drawn backdrop as you might expect,' Braben tells me. 'But the Milky Way and many of the stars around it are simply too bright and too uniform when compared to the real observable night sky.' Braben knew that the Milky Way appears somewhat dim when viewed from earth because of obscuring space dust, but he was surprised by the quantity of dust and absorbent matter that the team needed to add to the game world in order to match the real-world perspective.

'It appears as though our planet actually sits within that dust cloud, which is why the Milky Way appears so faint,' he says.

For Braben, it's also interesting how the dust cloud causes the night sky to drastically change appearance when you move only a hundred light years or so out of the galactic plane.

'At first, we see the familiar constellations begin to distort; some become unrecognisable quite quickly,' he says. 'Once you travel a hundred light years or more perpendicular to the plane, those constellations are long gone, and the galactic centre reveals itself more and more as your view emerges from the dust.'

Elite's model has expanded Braben's understanding of planet formation and distribution. Braben boasts that his games predicted extra-solar planets ('These were pretty close to those that have been since discovered, demonstrating that there is some validity in our algorithms'), and that the game's use of current planet-formation theories has shown the sheer number of different systems that can exist according to the rules, everything from nebulous gas giants to theoretically habitable worlds.

There may not be any practical application for Braben's game and its findings, but he nevertheless believes that it has significant value aside from science-fiction entertainment.

'The dust-cloud theory only became apparent when all the stellar information was included in the simulation,' he says. 'It shows that we can learn new things simply by looking at space holistically, rather than one element at a time.'

Elite: Dangerous collates a great deal of up-to-date astronomical information into one publicly available simulation, but Braben believes its true importance lies not in the accuracy of the model or its predictions but in its value as a story about the universe in which we live, the flowering sense of awe that, contrary to most narratives, grows with understanding and familiarity, rather than diminishes.

'If there is any practical application, then it is largely educational,' Braben tells me. 'But, most important, the game creates a sense of wonder based on what is truly out there.'

In *Minecraft* Mac has attempted to walk to the end of the world. In *Elite: Dangerous*, Braben has attempted to gather up the galaxy and squeeze it onto a desktop computer's hard drive, thereby making new discoveries about our solar system that challenge assumptions. In both cases the men are using the games as a way to explore new territory, to feel the thrill of the pioneer, pushing at the boundaries of our knowledge.

There is another video game that could never be fully charted or explored, one that has been specifically designed to be unimaginably vast in order that every player who enters its reality might always feel that sense of joy that comes from discovering something new, of being first.

Sean Murray, one of the creators of *No Man's Sky*, cannot guarantee that the virtual universe he is building is infinite, but he is certain that, if he's wrong, nobody will ever find out.

'If you were to visit one virtual planet in the game every second,' he says, 'then our own sun will have died before you'd have seen them all.' He smiles, conspiratorially: 'This means I can say that the *No Man's Sky* universe is infinite and nobody could possibly prove me wrong.'

No Man's Sky is a video game quite unlike any other. Developed for Sony's PlayStation 4 by an unfeasibly small team (as small as four members in the beginning, now only a dozen) at Hello Games, an independent studio in the south of England, it's a game in which every rock, flower, tree, creature and planet has been procedurally generated to create a vast and diverse play space which players can explore. 'We are attempting to do things that haven't been done before,' says Murray. 'No game has made it possible to fly down to a planet and for it to be planet-sized and feature life, ecology, lakes, caves, waterfalls and canyons, then seamlessly fly up through the stratosphere and take to space again. It's a tremendous challenge.'

Not only is this vision a technological challenge, it also bears the weight of unrivalled expectation. It's the game of so many childhood dreams. For Murray, that is truer than for most. His 'eccentric' family travelled a great deal when he was a child. He was born in Ireland, but the family lived on a farm in the Australian outback, away from civilisation.

'At night you could see the vastness of space,' he says. 'Meanwhile, we were responsible for our own electricity and survival. We were completely cut off. It had an impact on me that I carry through life.'

Murray formed Hello Games with three friends, all of whom had previously worked at major game-making studios, in 2009. When the team began to discuss what kind of game they would like to make, Murray returned to those formative memories under the stars.

'Those motions started to surface, the feelings you had as a child but which are only rarely displayed in video games,' he says. 'We talked about wanting to explore the vocations that we wanted to be when we were kids. These things were the most emotive for us.'

Hello Games' first project, *Joe Danger*, explored the life of one of these childhood dream roles: becoming a stuntman. The game was, according to Murray, 'annoyingly successful' in the sense that it locked the team into a cycle of sequels that they had formed the company to escape. During the next few years the team made four *Joe Danger* games for seven different video-game platforms.

'Then I had a mid-life game-development crisis,' says Murray. 'How many games did I have left? You do the math when you sit down to embark on a new project: will this be the next five, seven, ten years of my life working on this game? It changes your mind-set when a single game's development represents a significant chunk of life.'

With that existential crisis in mind, Murray decided it was time to embark upon the game he'd dreamed of as a child, a game about frontiership and existence on the edge of the unexplored.

'We talked about the feeling of landing on a planet and effectively being the first person to discover it, not knowing what was out there,' he says. 'In this era in which footage of every game is recorded and uploaded to YouTube, we wanted a game where, even if you watched every video, it still wouldn't be spoiled for you. And we wanted those discoveries to be meaningful in the sense that they could be shared with other players, all of whom existed in the exact same universe, rather than their own random dimension.'

All of that life and landscape is, as in *Elite*, generated from a 'seed' number (*Elite* used the Fibonacci sequence, while *No Man's Sky* derives its universe from one of the team's mobile phone numbers). In contrast to *Minecraft*, whose arrangement is different for every player, this 'seed' ensures that the universe is identical for every player, thereby giving the explorative experience meaning in the context of sharing. When a player discovers a new planet, or climbs that planet's tallest peak, they are able to upload the discovery to the game's servers, their name forever associated with the location, like a digital Christopher Columbus or Neil Armstrong.

'Players are even able to mark the planet as toxic or radioactive, or indicate what kind of life is there, and then that appears on everyone's map,' says Murray.

Experimentation has been a watchword throughout production. Originally, the game was randomly generated.

'The game would randomly pick the colour of the sky, then the terrain and so on,' he says. 'Only around one per cent of the time would it create something that looked natural, interesting and pleasing to the eye. The rest of the time it was a mess and, in some cases where the sky, the water and the terrain were all the same colour, unplayable.'

So the team began to create simple rules, layers of systems that interact and emerge.

'We have certain rules about the distance from a sun at which it is likely that there will be moisture,' explains Murray. 'From that we decide there will be rivers, lakes, erosion and weather, all of which is dependent on what the liquid is made from. The colour of the water in the atmosphere will derive from what the liquid is; we model the refractions to give you a modelled atmosphere.'

Similarly, the quality of light will depend on whether the solar system has a yellow sun or, for example, a red giant or red dwarf.

'These are simple rules but combined they produce something that's natural, recognisable to our eyes,' he explains. 'We have come from a place where everything was random and messy to something which is procedural and emergent, but still pleasingly chaotic in the mathematical sense. Things happen with cause and effect, but they are unpredictable for us.'

Not everything in *No Man's Sky* is unpredictable, however.

'We want to create a universe that functions on its own,' he says. 'It's up to you as to how you interact with the universe thereafter, but it functions without your input.'

For example, animals have daily routines, drinking in the lowland lakes during the daytime before retreating to the hills to graze. Likewise, hulking freighters plod through space to their own timetable. *No Man's Sky* is, like so many games, a nest of interlocking and parallel systems.

'They follow trade routes, visit planets and have smaller ships that peel off to gather resources. It's not possible to simulate that behaviour for an entire universe so we have fractal patterns they follow which are deterministic and parametric: they will always be the same.'

This combination of the predictable with the unknown is what makes exploration and discovery such a joy to humans. For the Elizabethan explorers, with their proud ships and dwindling supplies, there was the predictability of the world's systems wherever they went (the ebb and flow of the tides, the cycling of the sun and the moon, the power of the wind, the logical places to find meat, vegetables and fruit). But this familiarity was coupled with the promise of the unknown: the strange animals, the unpredictable local tribes, the unseen sights, and the rare pleasure of filling in a previously obfuscated area of a hand-drawn map.

Video games replicate this heady recipe for anyone with a controller and the necessary hardware. From familiar building blocks (quite literally, in the case of *Minecraft*'s brick-like construction) they create unfamiliar places with unfamiliar vistas that are, nevertheless, somehow real. It's telling that the latest video-game consoles have the built-in ability to take and share in-game photographs, an acknowledgement that visitors will want to capture a scene or a moment for posterity, to make their discoveries public and shared. Today, virtual places rival our world for beauty and diversity. There are the whispering deserts of *Red Dead Redemption* and the icy plains of *Super Mario 64*. There's Majula, a numinous clifftop homestead in *Dark Souls II*, a location seemingly chiselled from the rock over centuries by a ceaseless virtual wind. There's *Mass Effect*'s citadel, a colossal deep-space station as memorable as any city centre, and there are the buckshot islands of the Caribbean, exquisitely rendered as if from *Treasure Island*'s descriptive pages in *Assassins' Creed: Blag Flag*.

All of these places can be visited without the drag of real-world travel: the cumbersome luggage, the unreliable trains, the rude public, the sore feet. These vivid places have been compacted onto discs and hard drives, facilitating a kind of tourism and exploration that are convenient and danger-free. Can virtual discovery match the thrill of real-world exploration? As with success, the imitation is powerful, compelling and, crucially, cheaper and more accessible.

In the Taiwanese café, Rong-Yu may not have been drawn back to *League of Legends* by the promise of discovering some new virtual vista. After all, Summoner's Rift was a place he had visited many times before. But, like the traveller returning to a beloved locale, he would have grown to know the place, its contours, its plains and bushels, and, like the places we frequent in our daily existence, it would have become reassuringly familiar.

Perhaps this is the crucial point. The human urge to travel and to discover new places is almost universal. But behind that urge is a deeper need to arrive and, once there, discover a place that we can call our own and a place in which we belong.

05

BELONGING

INSERT COIN TO CONTINUE

The 1999 Electronic Entertainment Expo, or E3, a video-game conference held in Los Angeles, California, was a typically lavish, if bawdy, affair. Here, for three days, the world's video-game publishers gathered to show off their forthcoming titles to press and to purchasers in an overstimulating marketing circus. David Bowie performed at one of the conference's orbiting parties that week, and Bill Goldberg and some other glistening-skinned wrestlers grappled one another in a custom-built ring on the publisher EA's gargantuan booth. Away from the action of its main stage, EA had stationed a humble area advertising *The Sims*, an ambitious social-simulation project in which almost nobody outside of its development team believed.

For the publisher, one of America's longest-running makers and distributors of video games, *The Sims* was a legacy project, inherited when the company purchased the development studio, Maxis. *The Sims* had been in stammering development since 1993, when Will Wright, the celebrated designer of 1989's city-planning game *SimCity*, first had the idea for a simulation that would model human behaviour, not from the bird's-eye viewpoint of his earlier game (in which players could design, build and run a virtual city) but from the ground zero of domesticity.

But replicating the mundane dramas of the living room in game form had proved to be a challenge: *The Sims* was almost abandoned numerous times.

'We all knew that if we couldn't generate any interest at E3 that year, then the game would be cancelled for good,' Patrick J. Barrett III, one of the game's programmers, tells me. 'EA did nothing to help us. They hid us away. The game wasn't even displayed on the large screen with the other title's trailers.'

But, within hours, an unplanned kiss made *The Sims* the talk of the show.

Some video games offer us the chance to become other people or, at the very least, to experience something of the lives of others, be that of the motorsport driver who must negotiate Nürburgring's lingering corners in *Gran Turismo,* the intergalactic diplomat-cum-marine in *Mass Effect* or the border checkpoint clerk in *Papers, Please.* Here we are able to experience some of the challenges other people face, or the systems in which they operate, which differ from those of our own daily experience.

Others, like *The Sims,* offer us the chance to play as ourselves, or approximations of ourselves. In these games we are able to examine or rehearse our own lives, to take on the challenges that we face on this side of the screen, everything from paying off a mortgage to finding someone we care about with whom we want to spend the rest of our life.

In these video games (in which we are often given the opportunity to recreate our likeness on screen), it's important that our avatars closely reflect everything from our beliefs and values to our height and the colour of our hair. These games are not trying to generate empathy with another person so much as provide a space in which we might replicate ourselves on screen (albeit within the game's chosen parameters). In *Oblivion* or *Dark Souls* we can tweak the height of our avatar's eyebrows, the jut of the chin, the hairstyle and colour and so on, till we begin to see ourselves on screen. In *Rainbow 6* the technology takes care of much of the hard work for us: it takes a photograph of our face using a connected camera and pastes it onto a virtual mannequin to place us in the game. The designers of such games believe it's important that we can see ourselves in its reflection and that our most important characteristics are included in our virtual representation.

The Sims was the most fully formed attempt yet to allow players to approximate themselves (people known in-game as Sims), their family members, their love interests and many of the various contours of their real lives on screen. A broad scope was crucial to its success. Fail to represent the broad spectrum of types of human and the game would risk alienating potential members of the audience by essentially banning them from its reality. For the team at Maxis, that meant allowing players to pick an avatar that was tall or short, black or white, plump or thin. That meant, if the game was to be true to life, allowing players to adopt their sexuality.

During *The Sims*'s protracted development, the team debated whether to permit same-sex relationships in the game. If this digital Petri dish was to accurately model all aspects of human life, from work to play and love, it was natural that it would facilitate gay relationships. But there was also fear about how such a feature might adversely affect the game.

'No other game had facilitated same-sex relationships before – at least, to this extent – and some people figured that maybe we weren't the ideal ones to be first, as this was a game that EA really didn't want to begin with,' Barrett tells me. 'It felt to me like a fear thing.' After going back and forth for several months, the team finally decided to leave same-sex relationships out of the game code. It was, put simply, too risky.

When Barrett joined the company, in October 1998, he was unaware of the decision. A fortnight into his new job, he found himself with nothing to do when his supervisor, the game's lead programmer, Jamie Doornbos, took a short vacation. Jim Mackraz, Barrett's boss, needed a task to occupy his new employee, and he handed Barrett a document that outlined how social interactions in the game would work; the underlying rules for the game's AI that would dictate how the characters would dynamically interact with one another.

'He didn't think I could handle it with Jamie off on vacation, but he figured that at least I'd be out of his hair,' Barrett says. 'Neither he nor I realised that he'd given me an old design document to work from.'

That design document pre-dated the decision to exclude gay relationships in the game. Its pages described a web of social interactions, in which every kind of romantic relationship was permitted. That week, Barrett confounded the expectations of his boss. He successfully wrote the basic code for social interactions, including same-sex relationships.

'In hindsight, I probably should have questioned the design,' Barrett, who is gay, says. 'But the design felt right, so I just implemented it. Later, Will Wright stopped by my desk. He told me that he liked the social interactions, and that he was glad to see that same-sex support was back in the game.'

Nobody on the team questioned Barrett's work.

'They just pretty much ignored it,' he says. 'After a while, everyone was just used to the design being there. It was widely expected that EA would just kill it, anyway.'

In early 1999, before EA had a chance to kill the design, Barrett was asked to create a demo of the game to be shown at E3. The demo would consist of three scenes from the game. These were to be so-called on-rails scenes – not a true, live simulation but one that was pre-planned, and which would shake out the same way each time it was played, in order to show the game in its best light. One of the scenes was a wedding between two of the virtual characters.

'I had run out of time before E3, and there were so many Sims attending the wedding that I didn't have time to put them all on rails,' Barrett says.

On the first day of the show, the game's producers, Kana Ryan and Chris Trottier, watched in disbelief as two of the female Sims attending the virtual wedding leaned in and began to passionately kiss. The virtual characters had, during the live simulation, fallen in love. Moreover, they had chosen this moment to express their affection, in front of a live audience of assorted press.

Following the kiss, talk of *The Sims* spread through E3. Had the on-screen kiss been between two male characters, the reaction might have been different. But in the context of a marketing show that is dominated by straight men, the lesbian kiss worked in the game's favour.

'You might say that they stole the show,' Barrett says. 'I guess straight guys that make sports games loved the idea of controlling two lesbians.'

The ostensibly controversial design was overlooked owing to greater concerns about the project.

'EA was more worried that *The Sims* would flop and hurt the *SimCity* franchise by association,' says Barrett. 'It was also a different time; people weren't so violently for or against same-sex relationships. They didn't go out of the way to find it and react to it. The right-wing press didn't have the platform they have today to scream. There was no Twitter, no Facebook, no blogs. I kinda hoped people would come at night with pitchforks and torches. But it never happened.'

As a result, when *The Sims* finally launched, a player's character was free to fall in love with whomever the player chose, regardless of gender. For young gay players who were struggling to fit in the real world, the feature was profound. In the game, if not in life, they had found a place where they could be accepted.

Barrett kept the story of how same-sex relationships came to

The Sims a secret for more than a decade. In the years since *The Sims*'s original release, he believes, the world has changed in profound ways.

'At the time, it wasn't considered "normal" to be gay or lesbian,' he says. 'Some even saw it as dangerous. But in *The Sims* it was normal and safe to be a gay person. It was the first time we could play a game and be free to see ourselves represented within. It was a magical moment when my first same-sex Sims couple kissed. I still sometimes wonder how in the world I got away with it.'

When Barrett finally told his story in public, many who had played the game as teenagers shared their stories of the effect that being able to play as a gay character in the game had on them.

One user of the web forum Reddit wrote: 'Thinking back, it was actually the first way for me to explore my sexuality. I could be any gender I wanted, and I could date any gender I wanted.'

Another commentator wrote about the profound effect this simple design choice, almost included by accident, had on his sense of identity and belonging:

I was a fourteen-year-old closeted gay boy living in rural Kentucky when I played The Sims *for the first time. It's rare that a video game is a life-changing experience, but I'm not exaggerating when I say that it was. It was a safe place to experiment with social interactions that were absent from (if not illegal in) my real world. And it was a space free from the judgment, the ostracism, and the hate that was associated with homosexuality in my family and community. I still return to it from time to time for the sheer nostalgia. It was a little virtual neighbourhood that managed to make my world at the time seem so much bigger.*

In the design team's seemingly minor decision to reflect the fullness of life in the game, they gave players everywhere who previously felt as if there was no place for them in the world the sense that, just maybe, they had been wrong.

Video games, in their intoxicating recipe of theme, systems and fairness, provide a comfortable place where people can belong. Many characters are blank sheets, ready for us to project our own stories and ideas onto. It might seem curious to suggest that these virtual artifices, created from arcane lines of programming code and stitched textures, can provide a place of belonging. But there's an undeniable comfort in their judgement-less approachability (few who are physically able to interact with a video game are turned away – at least, not till the difficulty ramps up in the later stages) and, outside of the game worlds themselves, there's the ever-potent draw of a community of humans that share a common interest and enjoyment.

If you are a member of a marginalised group, what better salve could there be than a video game, which, at its best, is the great contemporary leveller? Games rarely distinguish between privilege and underprivilege, between rich and poor (the games that can be played for free, at least), between gay and straight, between loved and abused: once you enter their dimension, almost everybody is given an equal opportunity, the same blank sheet.

The sense of betrayal, then, when the 'community' around games does not reflect these qualities, or when games fail to adequately represent you, can be devastating.

There's a certain irony that *The Sims*, at least in part, gained same-sex relationships because of a reveal at E3. The event provides a sense of camaraderie and belonging for a certain type of person. But there are many who feel excluded by its tone, which primarily appeals to a young, white male demographic – something further reflected in many of the big-budget titles on show there. Indeed, E3 was forced to clean up its objectifying act a few years ago by the Californian state, which objected to game publishers' hiring of female models to attend their stands, usually in various states of undress.

At E3 in 2014, a male Microsoft representative told a female colleague during the company's press conference to 'just let it happen' as he attacked her when demonstrating the fighting game *Killer Instinct*. 'It'll be over soon,' he said, drawing a salacious comparison between his on-screen domination and a forced sexual encounter. 'I don't like this,' his colleague said in the reportedly improvised exchange, for which Microsoft later apologised.

Such moments create an exclusionary atmosphere, something that runs contrary to the endlessly welcoming potential of the medium. They imply that video games are only for a certain kind of player, principally white, Western, indoorsy teenagers. The cliché has proved indelible and even has its own name. 'Gamers' (a term that further segregates 'players', while adding ghost notes that call to mind the gambling industry) are routinely represented in the media as socially inept boys with poor hygiene and a proclivity for impotent rage, perhaps expressed down a Britney-style head mic while playing online shooters, or typed wrathfully onto an internet forum.

Gamers have, throughout the first thirty-odd years of their emergence, been depicted as the contemporary nerd group, a mildly downtrodden crowd, shunned by the jocks and achievers. Gamers are the losers who spend their days in darkened bedrooms furiously tapping on controllers or keyboards in a solitary pursuit that sits close to masturbation in the mind. There is, as ever, a degree of truth in the cliché, both in aesthetic and historical terms. Video games allow the people usually picked last to become top athletes; video games allow the bullied child a power fantasy in which they can overcome their attackers and triumph; video games offer clear routes to victory to people who struggle to achieve on the other side of the screen.

The stereotype is powerful and, while it presents non-gamers with an image of the typical player, also informs those who play games themselves. Many gain instruction as to how the world views them and the expectation, as is so often the case, becomes self-fulfilling: they play to type. The result has been that many of the medium's most staunch advocates and players view themselves as a certain type of person, perhaps wronged by society, for whom video games offer not only an escape but, more powerfully, a club in which they belong and triumph.

But while the cliché has endured, the context has shifted. Video-game players are not a homogeneous group, if indeed they ever were. The BBC estimates that 100 per cent of British teenagers play video games in some form or other. Within the next few decades, 'gamers' will be a term that encompasses every gay and transgender person, every girl and woman, every politician in the cabinet, everyone with a title in the House of Lords, every teacher, nurse, banker, dustman and social worker. Video games and their players will be acknowledged as ubiquitous, and the medium's commentators will be free to move from advocacy (the endless articles and television programmes that, beneath the angle, exist primarily to plead the case that games matter) to more rounded criticism.

But for now, gamers are dishonestly classed as a standardised tribe, and events such as E3 broadly reinforce the illusion. Who gains from maintaining the pervading stereotype? There is an argument to say that the game makers and publishers benefit: they are more easily able to target their marketing to a large and discrete group ('this is for the players', stated Sony's advertising campaign for its PlayStation 4 console, for example). But this isn't quite true: see Nintendo's gargantuan efforts to reach people outside of the traditional gamer demographic, including taking out advertisements in magazines such as *Saga* in an effort to appeal to retirees and octogenarians.

In truth, it's gamers who fit within the demographic who benefit the most: here, within the artifice of a 'community', they find a place to belong, a place where they fit, are understood and are free to be themselves and, together with like-minded people, enjoy a sense of collective power.

There is nothing deplorable about this; the urge to form groups with like-minded people is a universal one. But when that collective power is turned against those on the margins of the group, or those who present valid criticisms of its unifying subject (such as the American–Canadian feminist Anita Sarkeesian, who has been subject to everything from verbal abuse to threats of violence following her Tropes vs. Women series), it becomes problematic.

In 2014, the fears of certain elements of the self-described video-game community that their identity might be compromised coalesced into a movement of sorts, dubbed 'Gamergate' after a cringe-inducing Twitter hashtag popularised by the American actor Adam Baldwin. The Gamergate hashtag has been used more than a million times on Twitter, for myriad purposes. Some users denounced the kind of harassment that Sarkeesian has received, and consider the tag a demand for better ethical practices in video-game journalism, including more objective reporting and a removal of politics from criticism.

Most saw Gamergate as a hate movement, born of extremists, which has grown by providing a sense of belonging, self-worth and direction to those experiencing crisis or disaffection. The Gamergate movement is tiny relative to the mainstream audience for games, and its collective aims are ambiguous, but it has still managed to make itself heard. Outside of Twitter, the tag's users organised e-mail campaigns aimed at companies who advertise on gaming websites with whom they collectively disagree. After the industry website Gamasutra came under criticism for its condemnation of the hashtag, Intel removed advertising from the site. (Intel later claimed that it was unaware of the hashtag when it made its decision, but Gamasutra maintained that this is untrue. Intel ultimately apologised for pulling its ads and later reinstated them.)

Regardless of the aims and beliefs of any one individual who used the tag, Gamergate was (and continues to be) an expression of a narrative that certain video-game fans have chosen to believe: that the types of games they enjoy may change or disappear in the face of progressive criticism and commentary, and that the writers and journalists who cover the industry coordinate their message and skew it to push an agenda. It is a movement rooted in distrust and fear.

For those who have found a sense of belonging in video games, the fear is that criticism is the first step towards censorship. They worry that the games that have been meaningful to them will change. Some feel that Sarkeesian, in criticising games for their misogynistic portrayals of women, is also accusing those who enjoy the games of misogyny. Some believe that they are an oppressed minority.

And when the collective power of a group such as this is used to deny certain representations in games, or even the existence of certain subject matter within games, the medium is all the poorer. The remedy is, as always, education. Education establishes empathy, and video games are apt to participate in this work. They allow us to inhabit the shoes of 'others', to view the world through their eyes and to experience the challenges that they endure. This act is not only appealing, it's also educational.

Mattie Brice's *Mainichi* (2013), for example, offers an arresting glimpse into life as a mixed-race transgender person and the daily challenges faced (the daily taunts you endure en route to work each day soon force you to take the back roads in an effort to avoid confrontation). Games that explore this subject matter can help us understand the lives and challenges of other human beings. If executed well by the creator and absorbed properly by the player, these works can even have a transformative effect both for the individual and, in turn, the so-called 'community' of players that exists around games. The sense of belonging becomes richer and stronger, even as its more negative tribal aspects fade.

The power of video games is to give people a place to belong, to see themselves represented, to share their stories or even just to try out different ways of being. Indeed, the right game appearing at the right moment in a person's life can have a transformative effect, in much the same way as a book or film can reassure a person that they are not alone, that other people think like them or feel and experience similar things.

The difference, perhaps, is that a video game is a tangible place that can be visited, revisited and, in some cases, settled in. For some, the sense of belonging can be so great that they never want to leave . . .

Barloque was once a bustling virtual city.

Its streets were filled with a babble of voices. There were the residents who visited Joguer's Herbs and Roots store, the tourists who settled down for a tipple at the Browerstone Inn, the griping criminals en route to the old jailhouse.

Barloque is the capital of *Meridian 59*, the first computer game that allowed people from around the world to gather and quest together via the internet. At the peak of its popularity, soon after the game's release, in 1996, tens of thousands of players lived among its crudely rendered scenes filled with pixellated trees, shifting lava and tired mountains. They'd battle over resources, form and break alliances, loot and terrorise one another, and assume new identities for hours at a time. As with any place where humans gather, friendships and rivalries blossomed. Two players who met in Barloque were married: a relationship seeded in fantasy, consummated in reality.

Meridian 59 was the first 'massively multiplayer online game' (MMOG), a style of game that allows people from around the world to live and quest together in a shared virtual space via the internet. The idea for the game came from two brothers, Andrew and Chris Kirmse, who developed *Meridian 59* in the windowless basement of their parents' house, in Virginia. The game's title refers to its setting, the fifty-ninth provincial colony of an ancient empire.

More than twenty-five thousand people joined the game's public beta version, and the pair sold the game to the now defunct 3DO Company for five million dollars in stock. *Meridian 59* created the template that subsequent online worlds followed, but it enjoyed only a fraction of their success. The 3DO Company encountered financial difficulties in 2001, and sold the game's rights to two of the company's developers. They maintained the game as a commercial venture until 2009, but it was always a niche title.

Today, two decades after *Meridian 59*'s launch, Barloque's streets are quiet, its cobblestones buffed and rounded by little more than a digital breeze. They are rarely visited by more than twenty people in the world at any one time. With the release of each new MMOG, such as *World of Warcraft* (a game that, at the height of its popularity, had a population of more than twelve million), more residents left *Meridian 59*'s servers, an exodus inspired, as is

115

the case for so many émigrés, by the promise of a more interesting life, with greater opportunities – new types of monsters to do battle with, perhaps, or more vivid spells and bigger swords. A sense of belonging is what keeps people in a place. If the rest of the group moves on, the belonging goes with them and there's no reason left to remain.

But in *Meridian 59*, a spattering of faithful residents still remain. These players decided that their investment in this world was too great to give up and, in their collective decision to stay, they have settled together in a game that looks, to an outsider's eyes, technically crude and unwelcoming.

'I've tried to leave the game many times over the years,' says Tim Trude, a thirty-three-year-old player from Baton Rouge, Louisiana, who first started playing the game at the age of fifteen. 'But I always return. Some of these people I've grown up with. We have been enemies or friends for ever.'

Relationships are often key in keeping people rooted to a place, but for many of those left behind in *Meridian 59*, conflict is the glue that holds them there. Unlike most contemporary MMOGs, *Meridian 59* is focused on duelling. Players can attack one another unprovoked and, if they manage to defeat their opponents, collect their loot. The stakes in these battles are high.

'In most more recent MMOGs, death just means an inconvenient reset to a nearby starting point,' Andrew Kirmse, who is now a distinguished engineer at Google, tells me. 'Death in *Meridian 59* has real consequences, so people have to band together into guilds for protection. They form emotional attachments with both their friends and their enemies. We grew up on games where losing meant "game over". Just like in real life, we felt that some level of risk makes things more exciting. If there were nothing at stake, combat would be meaningless.'

Joshua Rotunda, a designer from New York who has played the game since he was fourteen, says that it's the high-stakes risk/ reward dynamic that first drew him in and continues to hold his interest. 'My friend and I began playing at the same time. Shortly after starting, my friend's character was attacked and killed in one of the main city streets by a gang of veteran players. Even though I was much weaker than them, and alone, I attacked the group. My friend quit the game, but I was fuelled with the need for vengeance in this little world and drawn in.'

Regardless of whether the inspiration to stay is friendship or rivalry, it seems to be the sense of community that keeps people playing *Meridian 59*. Samantha K, a twenty-seven-year-old from Oregon, who asked to remain anonymous in order to keep her virtual identity from her real-life friends, was introduced to the game by her parents. During the past thirteen years, she's tried some of the newer MMOGs, but she always returns to *Meridian 59*. 'I mostly enjoyed those other games,' she said. 'But, the worlds were so huge, it was hard to get to know anyone. I didn't know if I could trust people or not. *Meridian 59*'s smaller population keeps me going back. I know the game, and I know the people.'

Meridian 59's enduring population has also kept playing not only out of social obligation but out of grim necessity: if everyone left there would be no reason to keep the servers alive. 'You couldn't quit, really,' Matt Dymerski, an author from Ohio, and one of the game's best-known residents, says. 'The game needed you. All your friends needed you. If you didn't show up, the game would die.' Some nefarious players occasionally attempted to force the game's population to quit the game, in order to cause a type of virtual apocalypse. 'This actually happened four or five times in the game's ongoing life span,' Dymerski recalls. 'Each defeat generally required a huge update or change of ownership to draw the population back.'

These moments have formed part of an oral history, shared between players within the game and outside, on external forums. Dymerski refers to the 'great destruction of server 107', 'the subjugation of server 109', and so on. He plays infrequently today, but continues to contribute programming, tweaks and improvements to the code on which the world is built. Dymerski says that he stays put not only out of a sense of duty and community but also because he believes there are no satisfactory alternatives. 'While there are certainly bigger MMOGs, I'm not sure there were ever better games,' he says. 'So we remain on *Meridian 59*, fighting with the same two hundred people we've known all our lives, always waiting for that next big update that might "fix the game" and give us hope again.'

There's a tragic nobility to the game's codependent players. They are ostensibly kept here out of a sense of shared responsibility: if everybody leaves, *Meridian 59* will cease to exist. Nobody wants the end of the world on their conscience, even a vitual one.

But is that the truth? In 2012, the Kirmse brothers released the game's files as open source, so that anybody can play and join in the great work of improving the world. The decision essentially freed the game's population from having to reside there: the source files were public and, as such, the game would live on with or without its players.

And yet, still those players remain. Now Dymerski works to update the game with the Kirmses and a group of dedicated players. 'Even if everybody else left,' he says, 'I'd just keep adding new content for the next fifty years.'

In the next few years, the group hopes to bring *Meridian 59* to Steam, the most popular global digital game store, to introduce it to a new generation of players. Even if Barloque fails to attract new tourists, Dymerski believes that this outpost on the 'virtual periphery' will endure. For him, the sense of belonging is too great to abandon the place. It needs someone to reside there, to keep the memory alive and to keep building the memory.

06

EVIL

INSERT COIN TO CONTINUE

Nobody remembers their first kill. It's not like the high-security prison yards, where they pace just to forget. When it comes to video games, *nobody* remembers their first kill. If you can recall your first video game, well, then you've a chance of pinpointing the setting (over a blackened *Space Invaders* killing field? Atop a *Sonic the Hedgehog* green hill? Deep within a *Pac-Man* labyrinth?). But a name, date and face? Not likely.

It's not just the troubling number of digital skeletons in the players' closet that prevents recollection – although from *Super Mario* to *Call of Duty*, the trail of dead we virtual killers leave behind is of genocidal proportions. It's that these slayings are inconsequential and forgettable (there is the odd exception: the sight of the crack Russian markswoman Sniper Wolf's blood colouring the snow in *Metal Gear Solid*, for example, remains vivid in memory). Remember the first pawn or knight you 'took' in chess – the moment you callously toppled its body from the board? Hardly. Even if the piece had a name and backstory – a wife and children waiting on news back home, a star-crossed romance with a rival pawn – such details would have been forgotten the moment you packed away the board.

Most game murder leaves no imprint on the memory because it lacks meaning outside of the game context. Unlike depictions of death in cinema, which can trigger keen memories of the viewer's own past pains and sorrows, game violence is principally systemic in nature; its purpose is to move the player towards a state of either victory or of defeat, rarely to tears or reflection. Likewise, there is no remorse for the game murder, not only because the crime is fictional but also because, unless you're playing for money, there is no consequence beyond the border of the game's fleeting reality. And yet, to the casual observer, the player's blood-lust appears unnerving in both its flippancy and insatiability. Why are video games so unashamedly violent and why is virtual violence apparently so appealing to humankind?

Video games were deadly from the get-go. *Spacewar!* – the proto-game of the MIT labs played on $120,000 mainframe computers in the early 1960s – set the tone: a combative space game in which two players attempted to be the first to gun the other down. From this moment onwards violence was the medium's dominant mode.

The arcades concentrated the sport-as-combat metaphor into sixty-second clashes between player and computer, dealing as they invariably did in the violence of sudden failure. This was a decision driven by commerce, not art: their designers needed to kill off the player after a minute or so in order to make money. Violence was part of the business model: in the battle between human and machine, the machine must always overwhelm the player. In such games, as the author David Mitchell wrote in his novel *Number9Dream*, we 'play to postpone the inevitable', that moment when our own capacity for meting out playful death is overcome by our opponent's. But the obsession with screen violence isn't limited to the venerable arcade machines of the 1970s and 1980s. It seems to be within the DNA of all games, passed down from the playground (Cops and Robbers) to the board (Chess, Go) to, finally, the screen. Long-time video-game players are guilty of innumerable virtual crimes, from minor indiscretions like jaywalking, in Atari's *Frogger*, and smoking indoors, in *Metal Gear Solid*, to more serious outrages like driving under the influence, in *Grand Theft Auto IV*; gunning down an airport filled

with civilians, in *Call of Duty: Modern Warfare II*; and full-scale gen-
ocide in Sid Meier's *Civilization* series. In some cases, the appeal
specifically derives from the thrill of illicit behaviour.

The medium's core tenet – beat them before they beat you –
is so familiar that it passes almost unnoticed. From the dawn of
video-game time we have known to blast the Invaders before they
blast us, to swallow the fruit and chase the Pac-Man ghosts back
into a corner, to hoover up the health packs before our comrades
get to them, to cast the first stone, throw the first punch, make the
first headshot. This rule is part of the video-game contract, one
of the few human pursuits that, alongside sport, repels notions of
reconciliation or compromise.

We instinctively understand that our games are violent
because they reflect a violence within us as both individuals and
collectives. Games offer a way to explore violence within safe
and fictional borders, allowing us to confront our more primal
instincts. (Sony's *Tokyo Jungle* is a good example: it casts you as
an animal living in a post-apocalyptic vision of Japan's capital.
Regardless of whether you choose to play as herbivore or car-
nivore, your ambition is the same: crush the weak in order to
make yourself more powerful so that, in time, you or your offspring may crush the powerful. Just as *Minecraft* reminds us of
the mortal dread of a shelterless night, so *Tokyo Jungle* taps into
the ancient part of our brain that remembers what it is to shiver
under a tree, mad with hunger and an urgent desire to procreate
before it's too late.)

Besides, conflict is a necessary function of all fiction, including
games. So what, in 2013, inspired US president Barack Obama to
issue a call for Congress to fund a clutch of studies into video-
game violence's potential effects on the player? The problem
must be to do with the aesthetic of the violence – the way in
which it's rendered on the screen. It is a question of form, not

function – something that moves the conversation into the realm of all screen violence. It is a *style* concern.

Depictions of video-game violence chart a similar trajectory as those in cinema. They too have moved, generally, from the staid to the outlandish (from the 'ox-stunning fisticuffs', as Vladimir Nabokov put it, of 1940s-era Hollywood, to the gore of the contemporary slasher flick). But in video games the journey's pace was set by technology, not censorship. Early game designers couldn't spare the graphical processing power needed to render a spout of blood or a glistening wound. They made do with guttural screams to bring the collapsing pixels to more vivid life.

Devoid of censorship and drawn to the potential marketing potency of being dubbed a 'nasty', some developers even courted controversy with violent subject matter (notably 1982's *Custer's Revenge*, an Atari 2600 game in which players assume the role of a tumescent settler dodging arrows in a bid to rape a native American girl bound to a post). But even the most vulgar scene is robbed of its power when rendered in tubby pixels, like a lewd scrawl in a tittering teenage boy's exercise book.

Finally the technology caught up and games had the opportunity to begin to present the game violence and murders in something approaching a true-to-life form. Controversy was courted by savvy game publishers, who employed preposterously expensive publicists such as Max Clifford to whip the tabloids into a foam of indignation. But beneath the artificial outrage, the vividness of, say, *Grand Theft Auto*'s murder sprees, or *Call of Duty*'s spluttering death animations, made explicit the violence at the heart of games that had formerly been abstract or just implicit.

The new-found clarity of depictions of video-game violence brought the question of its potential effects on us into focus. To what extent is the video game's primal appeal based upon our baser instincts? And that question leads to another: to what extent does the video game's preoccupation with virtual violence affect us?

On 22 July 2011 Anders Behring Breivik, a thirty-three-year-old Norwegian man, bombed government buildings in Oslo, killing eight people. A few hours after the explosion he arrived at Utøya island, the site of a Norwegian Labour Party youth camp. He had posed as a police officer in order to gain entry to the ferry which would carry him to the island. When he disembarked he fired a Ruger Mini-14 semi-automatic assault rifle into the crowd of un-armed adolescents. Sixty-nine teenagers died in the attack.

After his arrest, Breivik explained that he had staged the politi-cal attack in order to save Norway and western Europe from a Muslim takeover, and that the Labour Party had to 'pay the price' for 'letting down Norway and the Norwegian people'. A few weeks later the Norwegian police made public Breivik's 'mani-festo' diary, in which he mentioned completing the fantasy role-playing game *Dragon Age: Origins*, using the online game *World of Warcraft* to relax, and, most worryingly, playing *Modern Warfare II* as part of his 'training-simulation' in advance of the attacks.

Since their inception games have struggled to shrug off the per-ception that they are violent, often mindless, occasionally sexist and fundamentally unconstructive. The medium's big-ticket blockbusters reinforce the viewpoint with their cacophonies and blooms of explosion. Video games may share DNA with chess, but their likeness is often that of adolescent power fantasy, glori-fying the war's aesthetic divorced from its graver consequences.

As a result of this perception, any public killing spree with a perpetrator under the age of forty or so throws a spotlight on video games and the question of whether their shadow falls across the story. Often, these headlines are generated in the cultural friction that exists between generations. On one hand, the game-literate – for whom video games have always been part of the entertainment diet. On the other, the video-game-illiterate, who mistrust video games for their ability to so forcefully and entirely distract young people from other works of art and life, and the way in which they render explicit the abstract violence of childhood games such as chess and Cops and Robbers.

Studies continue to be inconclusive as to whether there is a causal link between violence and consumption of violent media. In their 2010 paper 'Vulnerability to violent video games: a review and integration of personality research', published in *Review of General Psychology*, Patrick and Charlotte N. Markey showed links between raised aggression levels in players with a predisposition for violence when playing violent games. Another paper, 'Understanding the effects of violent video games on violent crime', published by the Social Science Research Network and reported by the *New York Times*, claimed to demonstrate a correlation between a drop in violent crime by youths, and the rise in popularity of violent video games. Despite the inconclusiveness of studies (which, it should be noted, have also never managed to establish a quantifiable link between the theatre, film or television and violence), numerous lawsuits have sought to implicate or even entirely blame the influence of video games for public acts of violence.

In the aftermath of the 1999 Columbine High School massacre in Colorado, the police eagerly pointed to perpetrators Eric Harris and Dylan Klebold's video-game hobby (Harris created his own levels for *Doom*, which were widely distributed). In 2001, relatives of the thirteen people killed in the massacre sought damages from computer-game makers, claiming their products helped bring about the killings. The lawsuit, which named twenty-five video-game publishers, including Sony, Activision, Atari and Nintendo, and sought $5 billion in damages, argued that investigations into the tragedy revealed the influence violent computer games had on the pair who carried out the shootings. The suit read: 'Absent the combination of extremely violent video games and these boys' incredibly deep involvement, use of and addiction to these games and the boys' basic personalities, these murders and this massacre would not have occurred.'

John DeCamp, the lawyer acting on behalf of the families, said the legal case was an attempt to change the marketing and distribution of violent video games that turn children into 'monster killers'. The judge dismissed the lawsuit, saying that computer games are not subject to product-liability laws.

Video-game supporters argue that critics have the causal link backwards, and that violent people are attracted to violent video games. Violent video games do not create violent people; they merely provide an escape for already troubled minds. The American psychologist Jerald Block argues that, following Harris and Klebold's arrest in January 1998 for theft, both youths had computer access restricted, which caused the anger that they had previously expressed in virtual worlds to spill into reality.

But when killers such as Breivik cite specific video games as being 'training tools' for their killing sprees, it becomes more difficult to dismiss the headlines, or to argue that the rote blaming of video games is nothing more than a straightforward attempt to confine madness with sense.

In context, the quotations from Breivik's diary were part of a general discussion of pastimes Breivik used to unwind, and crucially, came long after he had formed his initial plan for mass murder. This didn't stop British newspapers such as the *Mirror* claiming that *Call of Duty: Modern Warfare II* allows players to 'shoot people on an island', implying a causal link between the game and the style and location of the real-world killings. When Breivik testified to his fondness for *World of Warcraft* and his particular understanding of *Modern Warfare II* as a 'police shooting simulator', this led to headlines such as *The Times*'s 'Breivik played video games for a year to train for deadly attacks'.

But it's difficult to imagine how *World of Warcraft* could 'train' a person for any acts of violence, other than perhaps suggesting that murdering swamp rats is an effective way to pay for some fur-lined boots. More importantly, for many of its ten million monthly subscribers, it's an experience that creates community, provides the lonely with a virtual family and promotes teamwork and competition. *Modern Warfare II* is certainly thematically analogous to real-life shooting, but it is also as mainstream as a summer blockbuster; the game sold more than ten million copies in the US alone. In both cases, as with poker or golf, the games allow humans to play, compete and make social connections. They may improve hand-to-eye coordination, and in this sense could be used to 'train' one for murder, but less so than an obsession with clay-pigeon shooting might.

Video-game violence became America's concern *du jour* once again following the shooting at Sandy Hook Elementary School which occurred on 14 December 2012, in Newtown, Connecticut, when twenty-year-old Adam Lanza fatally shot twenty children and six adult staff members. The massacre, the deadliest at a high school or grade school in US history, renewed the debate about gun control in America. But video games were also an addendum to the post-Sandy Hook gun-control debate.

In December 2012, Wayne LaPierre, executive vice-president of the National Rifle Association, protested too much when he accused the games industry of being 'a callous, corrupt and corrupting shadow industry that sells and stows violence against its own people'. Then, in January 2013, representatives from Electronic Arts and Activision – the publishers behind the *Call of Duty* and *Medal of Honor* series – were called into a conference with Vice-President Joe Biden to discuss the relationship between games and real-life violence. Subsequently President Obama has called for more studies to investigate what links tie game violence to real violence, while US senator Lamar Alexander provided the extremist perspective when he proclaimed on television that 'video games are a bigger problem than guns'.

Overstated depictions of violence are not unique to video games and cinema. Shakespeare's theatres swilled with blood, and directors routinely used goat's entrails to add gore to a scene. If the realistic (or exaggerated) depiction of violence in art leads to real-world mimicry, then it's been happening for centuries. As the British comedian Peter Cook drolly put it, when referring to the supposed copycat effect of screen violence: 'Michael Moriarty was very good as that Nazi on the television. As soon as I switched off the third episode, I got on the number eighteen bus and got up to Golders Green and . . . I must've slaughtered about eighteen thousand before I realised, you know, what I was doing. And I thought: it's the fucking television that's driven me to this.'

Trying to rationalise the irrational leads to a madness of its own. But beyond the sensationalism, it's more difficult to explain away the disproportionate focus on violent content, a point that few of video gaming's apologists bring up. Hollywood may share an obsession with bullets and explosions, but cinema's thematic range is more diverse, offering romance, drama and documentary – subjects that games struggle to depict.

Is this merely a by-product of the medium's own prolonged

adolescence? As games such as *Papers, Please* and *Cart Life* demonstrate, game designers who have begun to explore away from the plainer themes of competition and domination (which are so fundamental to the commercial behemoths, *Call of Duty*, *FIFA* et al.) are beginning to find more widespread success. Or do video games, as in Block's assertion, principally allow us to vent our anger, our primal instincts of violence, in a safe space, without consequence?

Is some of the appeal of video games the way in which they allow us to explore our own darkness? Or is it something else? Do games enable us to explore the violence around us as an act of processing and understanding?

Before Jewish families were sent to the labour and extermination camps during the Second World War, they were placed in ghettos to await processing. Here, according to survivors' accounts, parents tried to divert their children's attention from the surrounding horror by creating makeshift playgrounds. These play spaces were intended to preserve and maintain not only a kind of routine amid the dread disruption, but also a place of innocence.

Adults also sought out avenues for play, especially the kind of games that would offer them a psychological reprieve from their circumstances. The historian George Eisen recounts one story in his book *Children and Play in the Holocaust* of a man who traded a crust of bread for a chessboard. By playing chess, he reasoned, he could forget his hunger.

The children used to play in a different way: not to escape their reality, but to confront it. Their games were, typically, violent and warlike. They played games that, according to Eisen, simulated 'blowing up bunkers', 'slaughtering' and 'seizing the clothes of the dead'. At Vilna, Jewish children played a game they dubbed

'Jews and Gestapomen'. The children playing the role of Jews would overpower their tormenters and beat them with sticks, which were used to represent rifles.

Play was also found in the extermination camps, where children who had the strength to move reportedly created a game they dubbed 'tickling the corpse'. At Auschwitz-Birkenau they dared one another to touch the electric fence and, most grimly of all, they played 'gas chamber', in which players threw rocks into a pit while mimicking the screams of the dying.

One game, 'klepsi-klepsi', replicated the physical abuse Jews often experienced during daily roll call. One player would be blindfolded while another stepped forward to strike him on the face. Then, with blindfold removed, the one who had been hit would guess which of the children was his attacker, judging their guilt from their behavioural clues. To survive Auschwitz, Eisen points out, one often had to bluff about stealing bread or about knowing of someone's escape or resistance plans. Klepsi-klepsi was a rehearsal.

Peter Gray, a developmental psychologist, explains in his book *Free to Learn* why this kind of play was important to the children of the camps, and why violent-themed play continues to be valuable outside of that extreme context:

> In play, whether it is the idyllic play we most like to envision or the play described by Eisen, children bring the realities of their world into a fictional context, where it is safe to confront them, to experience them, and to practice ways of dealing with them. Some people fear that violent play creates violent adults, but in reality the opposite is true. Violence in the adult world leads children, quite properly, to play at violence. How else can they prepare themselves emotionally, intellectually, and physically for reality? It is wrong to think that somehow

we can reform the world for the future by controlling children's play and controlling what they learn. If we want to reform the world, we have to reform the world; children will follow suit. The children must, and will, prepare themselves for the real world to which they must adapt to survive.

Despite the fact that violent play is usually a symptom of violent society, a way to understand through fiction the bruises of reality, video games are the latest recruit to the aftermath blame tradition. And, like all new mediums, they provide the right sort of scapegoat, enjoyed as they are by a generally younger demographic, from whose ranks America's school shooters have often stepped. They are separated from older media by virtue of their interactivity. The medium has a unique capacity to inveigle, and even implicate, its audience through its interactivity. When we watch a violent scene in a film or read a description of violence in a novel, no matter how graphic it is, we are merely spectators. In video games, whose stories are usually written in the second person singular – 'you,' rather than 'he' or 'she' or some foreign 'I' – we are active, if virtual, participants. Often the game's story remains in stasis until we press the button to step off the sidewalk, light the cigarette, drunkenly turn the key in the ignition, or pull a yielding trigger.

If video games can prepare us to become expert accountants or city planners or drivers by mimicking these real-life activities, it's logical to argue they might also prepare us for crime and violence.

But as the examples of the extermination camps demonstrate, games tend to reflect and replicate the world in which they are designed. They present a safe and consequence-less space in which to enclose and examine human life, love and tragedy. No wonder they can be so elementally appealing, when they aid us in understanding the confusion and mess of existence.

If this is true, then, in games as in all fiction, anything is permissible (so long as we also uphold the rule that nothing is beyond criticism). Video games should, by that measure, be free to replicate any human tragedy – perhaps even one of the school shootings for which they have so often shared blame.

Danny Ledonne released his independent game *Super Columbine Massacre* in April 2005. The game's cutesy, sixteen-bit *Final Fantasy*-style graphics belie its macabre and challenging content: in the game you play as Harris and Klebold, following their actions on the day of the Columbine High School attack.

Ledonne was attending another high school in Colorado at the time of the killings. Confused as to why boys of a similar age, location and situation (he, like Harris and Klebold, was bullied at school) would express themselves in such a destructive manner, Ledonne decided to make a home-brew video game using the PC program *RPG Maker* to try to make sense of the events leading up to and during that day.

The plotline follows the events of the day with meticulous detail amassed from newspaper reports and sheriff records. Such attention to minutiae (your characters have the exact same number of bombs and weapons as Harris and Klebold, for example) has seen Ledonne described as obsessional, perhaps even glorifying the attackers' acts.

'I felt like if I wanted to make a serious game, I ought to take my subject seriously,' says Ledonne. 'This wasn't going to be something I'd sink months of time into unless I was going to tell the story the way it happened. Without the attention to detail, I think the game would run a much greater risk of trivialising the shooting and would undermine the game's primary purpose of showing the player a story they only thought they knew before.'

While the game doesn't show footage or stills of any of the victims, it does intersperse real photographs of the boys, quote things that they said and, finally, displays a graphic image from the coroner's office of their lifeless bodies at the scene. What drove the decision to display such an image?

'That decision was an easy one,' says Ledonne. 'I wanted to connect the limited graphical reality of the "game" with the deeply serious consequences of the game's subject matter. They killed people. They killed themselves. This isn't *Mario Bros*. This really happened. Here are the crime-scene photos to prove it. The player must now account for what has happened thus far in the game. I felt like a documentary approach filled with real quotations and real photos was the best way to confront the shooting in honest terms. Video games often sanitise their violence and thereby short-change the player in terms of understanding the ramifications of his/her actions. I wanted to challenge that. This is a subject that demanded as much.'

The game quietly launched on the internet for download on 20 April 2005, the sixth anniversary of the shootings. For a while it went mostly undiscovered, but when the academic Ian Bogost wrote about the game in May 2006 it began to gain attention and notoriety. Many press outlets decried the game for making entertainment out of others' suffering. Ledonne is adamant that this is not the case.

'I don't regard this game as entertainment,' he says. 'Many have written about how morally challenging this game is to play. A review in Salt Lake City said: "I hate this game with all my heart not because it was made, but because the real Columbine massacre occurred." And, that, I think, is the real point.'

Like the horrors reflected in the children's games of the camps, Ledonne's game aimed to make some sense of the atrocity, or at least to provide a crude route towards understanding and empathy. Its primary purpose is to give the player an experience of the lives the pair led, the horrific and tragic acts they perpetrated, and their eventual demise at their own hands. It aims to provide players with the killers' perspective – their feelings of alienation and loneliness, their withdrawal into an isolated world in which they used media – including video games, but also music and books – to rekindle their feelings of alienation.

As Bogost put it: 'This game is certainly not meant to make us excuse Harris and Klebold, or to forgive them. But it does ask us to empathise with them, to try to understand the situation they perceived themselves to be stuck in.'

In this sense the game shares an ambition with Michael Moore's *Bowling for Columbine* and Gus Van Sant's *Elephant*, films which respectively dissect and recreate the events at Columbine, and which were awarded the Palme d'Or in consecutive years. Ledonne's game, by contrast, was banned from an awards event. In October 2006, Sam Roberts, the Guerilla Gamemaker Competition director of the independent Slamdance film festival, emailed Ledonne encouraging him to submit the game to the contest. Ledonne agreed to submit his game as he considered the award's existence as evidence that 'all forms of art can be valid tools for societal exploration (even painful topics like school shootings)'. The game was shortlisted for the award until, a few weeks later, the event's organiser, Peter Baxter, announced the game's removal.

The festival organisers blamed the decision on fear that a media backlash against the game's inclusion could scare off sponsors, or even attract a civil lawsuit, something that could throw the festival's future into jeopardy. The decision drew condemnation from many who believe video games have the power to investigate violence, not just as a mode of interaction, but as a real-world topic.

'There are moments in the game that push the idea that games can be emotionally difficult, that they can be satire, that they can be critical social commentary,' says Ledonne. 'If all people want is entertainment, this isn't a very good choice; the graphics are sub-par at best, the gameplay is clunky and limited, and there is so much reading involved that someone looking for a "murder simulator" would best look elsewhere. But entertainment aside, is it "wrong" to make a film that centres on another's suffering? What about a book? A painting? A song? A theatre production? Why are games different? If there are films about the suffering of Christ, why could there not be video games? Video games absolutely should be able to approach the same issues other art forms do albeit in the manner that is inherently unique to gaming.'

It's this 'inherently unique' aspect to video games that is the cause of so much consternation when it comes to their depicting sensitive issues and events. While *Bowling for Columbine* and *Elephant* addressed many of the same issues as Ledonne's game, there is a key difference, in that here you role-play as the antagonists.

'I disagree with the contention that because video games are interactive they must somehow be treated differently to other creative media,' argues Ledonne. 'This is a dangerous line of argument because of course every medium is in some way distinct from the others. Surely this tired concern about how "interactive" games are is merely a reaction to their infancy as a medium. I can't think of a single medium that hasn't had a share of controversy for whatever unique expressive qualities it has.'

Ledonne points out that similar criticisms of tabletop role-playing games like *Dungeons & Dragons* were made in the 1970s.

'I suppose the same arguments could be wheeled out against an actor who plays an antagonist or children playing Cops and Robbers,' he says.

Bogost agrees: 'Interactivity is one of the core features that differentiate games from passive media like film. In a game we play a role. Most of the time, the roles we play in games are roles of power. Space marine, world-class footballer or hero plumber. Isn't it about time we played the role of the weak, the misunderstood, even the evil? If video games remain places where we only exercise juvenile power fantasies, I'm not sure there will be a meaningful future for the medium.'

The idea that video games can allow a player to take on the role of an antagonist is not a new one. The difference with Ledonne's game is that the position is forced upon you as you recreate real-life horrors. Why recreate historical tragedy, when there is less risk of wounding people who were affected by the real events within fiction?

'We can learn about the system of ideas, values, historical circumstances, and personal feelings that drove their decisions,' explains Bogost. 'I'm sure every American wonders how and why the 9/11 hijackers could choose to commit the acts they did. Is it enough just to wonder? Should we not try to understand? Understanding and empathy does not mean apology or excuse. It's worth flipping this point on its head: from the hijackers' perspective, what do you think someone can learn by playing a game in which people value global capitalism over faith? In which people can learn to become soldiers of America's Army to pursue that goal? Who gets to be right?'

'Games offer a window through which we can see the world a different way,' says Ledonne. 'I suppose that's a lofty jump for some people to make and as a result video games are often scrutinised because the power of role-playing can be very potent. But I think this is something to study, redefine, and embrace . . . not flee from.'

Custer's Revenge, the game for the Atari 2600 launched in 1982, gained notoriety for casting the player as General Custer, the historical figure who, in the game, is tasked with overcoming various obstacles in order to rape a Native American woman bound to a post. The game received widespread criticism, and raises the question of whether meaningless evil can be validly portrayed in games.

'We shouldn't confuse expression with sensationalism and offence,' says Bogost. '*Custer's Revenge* was probably created to offend, not to inspire or raise questions in its players. That is not because it depicts rape, by the way, but because it fails to offer any meaningful perspective on rape, from a historical perspective, from the perspective of the perpetrator, or from the perspective of the victim.'

'It's important to remember that while *Birth of a Nation* is a deeply racist film by today's standards, it is also an important landmark for film-making itself,' says Ledonne. 'Perhaps the same importance cannot be placed on *Custer's Revenge* but nonetheless perspectives of sexism and racism should have the same accessibility in video games as they do in a variety of other mediums. Watching *Triumph of the Will* or listening to Nirvana's "Rape Me" can be very valid experiences for an audience to have. So long as an issue exists in the real world, artists will feel compelled to represent it in their work . . . including via video games.'

Yet video games' detractors seem nervous about ascribing such freedoms to the medium, or celebrating them. Video games involve play and play is associated with childhood. For that reason, even subconsciously, many struggle to accept true creative freedom in terms of the medium's subject matter.

'If games are to truly explore the world we live in instead

of merely allowing us to escape from it whenever we press the power button, then games need to have the artistic licence to approach any subject,' says Ledonne. 'I think it is possible to make a game on virtually any topic that comes to mind and the game should be evaluated on its content rather than its form. Is there any subject matter that should be off limits for sculpture or acrylic? Of course not. What matters is what the work contains.'

Bogost agrees: 'No topic is off limits to art of any kind. We must not be afraid to try to understand our world, even if such progress seems difficult or dangerous. Clearly there are more and less meaningful ways to simulate any topic. But no subject is a priori off limits. It is then the job of the critic to tell us whether it is good or successful.'

Whether or not there should be limits to fiction is not a new question. It was Vladimir Nabokov's wife, Véra, who rescued the manuscript of *Lolita* from a backyard incinerator at Cornell University. Beset by doubt over the book's subject matter, which examines an older man's infatuation with a teenage girl, Nabokov hoped to burn the novel before it reached the public. Likewise, the American literary critic George Steiner had second thoughts on the publication of his 1981 novella *The Portage to San Cristobal of A.H.*, in which Adolf Hitler survives the Second World War and is given the opportunity to defend his crimes. Steiner had the book recalled and pulped.

The question of whether – or to what extent – literature should allow readers into the minds of terrorists, murderers and abusers both fictional and historical is one that continues to trouble authors. But if video-game creators share such qualms it hasn't stopped the production, in the course of the past forty years, of games that ask players to march in the boots of legions of despots and criminals, both petty and major.

Most would agree that no topic is off limits in games, even if examples of games that have tackled difficult territory with grace and assurance are scarce. But in games the author doesn't always control the action. Players are often given free will, even the free will to act out unspeakable evils that the game's creator may not be able to present in context or with appropriate virtual consequence.

This becomes a greater issue in games that present not carefully authored stories to follow, but rather entire systems in which the player is free to behave in ways of their own choosing. In 2013, in anticipation of the release of *Grand Theft Auto V*, a forum participant asked whether players would be able to rape women in the game. In the post, which was widely shared and condemned on social media, he wrote, 'I want to have the opportunity to kidnap a woman, hostage her, put her in my basement and rape her everyday, listen to her crying, watching her tears.' When our world facilitates this kind of behaviour (and attaches to it grave consequences), should a game not be allowed to do the same in its careful imitation?

A 2011 Supreme Court ruling recognised that video games, like other forms of art and entertainment, are protected by the First Amendment as a form of speech.

'For better or worse,' Supreme Court Justice Antonin Scalia wrote in the decision, 'our society has long regarded many depictions of killing and maiming as suitable features of popular entertainment.' As such, the vision of opportunity expressed in that rather worrying forum post is permissible. But if this freedom is necessary to maintain the artifice of the world, it can be argued that the designer has a responsibility to engineer the virtual victim's reactions in order to communicate something of the pain and damage inflicted.

Fictional characters, whether they appear in novels, films or video games, are never fully independent entities. They are conjured by words on a page, directions in a screenplay, or lines of programming code, existing only in imagination or on a screen. A creator has no moral obligation to his or her fictional characters, and in that sense anything is theoretically permissible in a video game. But a game creator does perhaps have a moral obligation to the player, who, having been asked to make choices, can be uniquely degraded by the experience. The game creator's responsibility to the player is, in Kurt Vonnegut's phrase, not to waste his or her time. But it is also, when it comes to solemn screen violence, to add meaning to its inclusion.

Questions about video-game violence will continue to gain urgency. History has shown that the video-game medium curves towards photorealism. As the fidelity of our virtual worlds moves ever closer to that of our own, the moral duty of game makers arguably intensifies in kind. The guns in combat games are now brand-name weapons, the conflicts in them are often based on real wars, and each hair on a virtual soldier's head has been numbered by some wearied 3-D modeller. The go-to argument that video games are analogous to innocuous playground games of Cops and Robbers grows weaker as verisimilitude increases. How much more repellent might *Custer's Revenge* be if rendered by contemporary technologies with their ever-more-realistic graphics?

The rise of motion control (where physical gestures replace traditional button-control inputs in video games) and virtual reality (which fool our minds into thinking we have bodily entered into a virtual space and role) will, for many, accentuate those concerns. Some games now no longer merely require your mind and thumbs, but also your entire body. In a hypothetical motion-controlled video-game version of *Lolita*, it would be possible to inhabit the body, as well as the mind, of protagonist Humbert Humbert. A virtual sex crime might elicit a very different response if, instead of pressing a button to instigate it, you were required to mimic its pelvic thrusts and parries – even if, as in Nabokov's work, it was included to illustrate or illuminate, not titillate.

In the aftershock of an act of madness some seek prayer, others revenge – but most seek sense in the senseless moment.

In the hours following the Sandy Hook massacre, a news outlet erroneously reported that the shooter was Ryan Lanza, the brother of gunman Adam Lanza. Poring over his Facebook profile, many noticed that Ryan had 'liked' the video game *Mass Effect*. Emboldened by an expert on Fox News drawing an immediate link between the killing and video games, an angry mob descended on the developer's Facebook page, declaring them 'child killers'.

Despite the absurdity of the logic, a chain effect was set in action, one that's ended up at the White House. Video games are the youngest creative medium. What literature learned in four millennia, cinema was forced to learn in a century and video games are now expected to have mastered in three decades.

The issue of game violence and its potential effects may seem like an abstract, esoteric issue, demanding scientific study to make clear what is opaque. But game violence has logic and precedence and is always an act of play, not of sincerity. The worry is, then, those who cannot tell the difference, from disturbed high-school student to the US senator.

07

EMPATHY

INSERT COIN TO CONTINUE

The brittle bark of rifle fire rattled the back of Mitch Swenson's teeth. If the guards had shot to scare rather than to wound, the warning had its intended effect. As he sprinted across a Turkish field, Swenson, a twenty-six-year-old journalism student at Columbia University, was 'utterly terrified', as he puts it today. As he and his three accomplices pressed through a hole in the fence and padded into an unexpectedly peaceful Syrian pomegranate orchard, the relief was palpable, even if it was short-lived.

This was not, as Swenson puts it, his 'first rodeo'. Two years earlier, in 2011, the young journalist was present in Cairo's Tahrir Square on the first day of the revolution that helped instigate the Arab Spring, the wave of revolutionary protests that spread across the Middle East, unseating rulers in its wake. Since then he's visited a clutch of troubled nations: Libya, South Sudan and the Congo. He's 'been around men with guns before'. Even so, this autumn night, clammy with cloud and heat, saw him enter a different kind of battle. 'Syria is a type of conflict that humanity has never really seen before,' he says. 'All of the rules are out of the window.'

For the next ten days Swenson and his partners (David Axe, the founder of *War is Boring*, a blog that covers war zones, a photographer and a local fixer) travelled with members of the Sham Falcons Brigade, a group of rebels opposed to the Syrian president Bashar al-Assad and his troops, the Syrian armed forces. Few foreign journalists have remained in the country; the dangers are extreme. The preceding day two Spanish journalists were kidnapped while preparing to leave the country (they were eventually released in March 2014). During his brief time reporting in the country Swenson interviewed soldiers and smugglers and saw first-hand what he describes as an 'all-consuming, merciless and heart-eating machine of war'. Then, on 4 October, Swenson left Syria. He was due to start at college the following week.

When he landed in New York, Swenson began to write about his experiences. But the prose failed to capture the urgency of the chaos and distress he had witnessed (or, at least, failed to stand out from other similar reports written by foreign journalists). Moreover, he shared a challenge with many an overseas news reporter: how to interest readers in a faraway nation and its remote problems, ostensibly unconnected to their own.

Swenson decided to move from written reportage to something entirely different: video-game reportage. The medium has often been used to replicate vivid historical and futuristic battlefields, but rarely to present contemporary war journalism. Swenson's logic was sound: if readers struggle to engage with stories of the lives of ordinary people living in fear and anguish on the other side of the world, perhaps they will empathise if asked to live out a day or a week in their shoes. Maybe a video game, which moves the player from passive spectator to active protagonist, would communicate something of the urgency that he had felt there, running across that field.

The journalist describes 1,000 Days of Syria, which is freely available to play on the internet, as 'part electric literature; part newscast and part choose-your-own-adventure', a reference to the young adult fiction books popularised in the 1980s in which readers can alter the direction of the plot by making simple decisions for the protagonist and turning to the applicable page. In the game, you play as three characters: a foreign photojournalist, a mother living in Daraa, a city in south-western Syria, just north of the border with Jordan, and a young rebel living in Aleppo. Each character is a fictionalised amalgam of people Swenson met on his travels. The story is delivered in disparate chunks of narrative text and, at the end of each excerpt, you make choices about what your character will do next: will you attempt to flee the country or stay put? How will you try to pass the time when you're imprisoned in a dimly lit cell?

Each character has three possible endings and, at times, their stories intersect. Swenson attempts to weave together Syria's story with his trio of individual, semi-fictionalised narratives. While, in his attempt to explain the first three years of the Syrian conflict, Swenson relies on lengthy exposition, the tales are at times affecting, not least because they are in part based upon his own experience, and the experience of those he interviewed first-hand in the country. In his endeavour Swenson discovered something fascinating. A televised news report in which the camera pans across a pocked Syrian street before, say, entering a building in which a huddle of displaced Syrians mourn and tremble is undeniably affecting. But a video game that casts us as one of those Syrians is moving in an entirely different sort of way. Here we are no longer spectators to the horror. We are, for a moment, its subject.

During a panel discussion at the USC School of Cinematic Arts in 2013, the film director Steven Spielberg said of video games, 'The second you pick up the controller, something turns off in the heart. It becomes a sport.' Spielberg's assertion is often true. There is, as we have seen, a sporting component to most video games that can, if focused on to the exclusion of all else, place us in a psychological mode of competition. This, in Spielberg's phrase, turns something off in the heart.

But this is a half-truth. Video games contain challenge, but that challenge is also usually framed in the language of human drama, something that quickens the human heart. In *Super Mario* the challenge is to reach the far end of the screen, but it's framed as a hostage-rescue mission. In *SimCity* the challenge is to create an elegant engine powered by a network of motors and cables but it's framed as an exercise in city planning.

Star Wars director George Lucas, whose company LucasArts produced seminal story-based games throughout the 1990s and who was present on the same panel as Spielberg, had a different opinion to his peer.

'The big game of the next five years will be one in which you empathise strongly with the characters through a love story,' he said. 'That will be the *Titanic* of the games industry, because you have actual relationships on screen instead of people being shot.'

Creating paced and plotted stories in games where the protagonist often has a degree of free will is a unique challenge but the medium undeniably excels in its ability to recreate the environments that facilitate stories in the first place. Games are able to render in exquisite detail places and points in history, as well as, if they so choose, their societal systems. Then, by placing us in the active role of a protagonist in a story, with our own agency and limited freedoms, they allow us to experience lives, places and circumstances that differ from our own.

Where a documentary or written piece of journalism tries to generate empathy with a character through sharing their own words, images and stories, a video game has an additional dimension. It is able to cast us as the subject, or, at least, to position us where we are able to experience life from that person or group's perspective, with their unique set of privileges or setbacks. For Walt Whitman, this ability to empathise with another character's situation was the key to powerful storytelling. 'I do not ask the wounded person how he feels,' he wrote, 'I myself become the wounded person.'

Video games move this act of 'becoming' another from the realm of the imagination to the more tangible realm of the screen and controller. They cast us as the subject, where we cannot help but see things, in literal terms at least, from their perspective.

Swenson's project derived from a straightforward question. If it's possible for a video game like *Papers, Please* to generate empathy with a passport-control clerk at the borders of a fictional eastern European country, or for a game like *Super Columbine Massacre RPG* to attempt to generate empathy with high-school killers, then surely a game can generate empathy and understanding of those who face real-world difficulties in the same way? It's an approach that independent studios like Molleindustria are exploring in fascinating ways, with games such as *Oiligarchy*, in which you play as the executive of an oil multinational, exploring and drilling around the world, corrupting politicians and blocking alternative energies, and *Phone Story*, which examines the plight of sweatshop workers assembling smartphones for their factory's Western clients. (In 2012 the studio donated $6,000 to Tian Yu, a nineteen-year-old girl who suffered serious injuries after trying to commit suicide by jumping from Foxconn's factory complex where she was working in 2010.)

As anyone who has played an unbalanced multiplayer video game in which two factions face off against one another can attest, games are also well suited to illustrate systemic injustice. If you are assigned to the stronger faction's side you benefit from the systemic imbalance (for example, you might have more powerful abilities, more useful resources, or a better strategic position on the map). You didn't ask for this advantage (in fact, the unfairness might even annoy you, as victory isn't necessarily founded on merit). But you benefit nonetheless – even if you find yourself losing the game. This is a useful and powerful illustration of the kind of privileges that affect the real world, giving some a great advantage over others, often through nothing more than the accident of their birth, the family, race or location into which they were born.

It's not only the complex social and industrial systems of power that can be illustrated by video games. The creator of the webgame *10 Seconds in Hell* uses the medium to communicate the abject terror of the domestic-abuse victim. The game, freely available on the internet, places you in a locked room ten seconds before your violent partner enters. You have this tiny window in which to explore your options, to find a way to evade the seemingly inevitable. The sense of horror and hopelessness in your predicament is powerfully illustrative, and it's all communicated in a few seconds.

Actual Sunlight is an unflinching examination of the causes of suicide, and the feelings of paralysis, self-loathing and long-term destruction that can result from depression. *Dsy4ia* is a short interactive story about the process of undergoing hormone replacement therapy. It attempts to replicate the confusion, fear, doubt and societal suspicion that transgender people can experience through the visual language of games (for example, you have to place *Tetris* blocks in a play area where none of them fit).

Shelter is a game about a family of badgers that manages to explore the human condition better than most. It is a game about custody, about being the carer of things smaller and weaker than you. It draws upon those maternal or paternal anxieties that stretch down, past the conscious mind, to something deeper and more primal. Your aim is straightforward and ancient: lead your offspring to shelter, keep them safe, keep them fed. And when you fail in that aim – when you fail as a parent in your most important duty – the grief is close to unbearable.

It's this unique power of games to place us at the epicentre of real-world drama (one that game makers are only just beginning to explore) which led Swenson to consider a game for his report-age, as opposed to traditional non-interactive storytelling.

'I was able to incorporate some of the details from my note-books into the historical non-fiction aspect of the game that were not pertinent to reporting,' he says. 'In that way I could tell more of a full-bodied experience of what's going on there.'

Then, by placing the player in the role of these characters, with a certain degree of agency, empathy and connection are built in a different way to how they are in linear media such as film and literature.

We may question the quality of *1,000 Days of Syria*'s execution (there is a large amount of exposition which can be a slog to work through), but it's a useful early example of how interactive story-telling can be an interesting and effective way to report on real-world events and to illuminate humanity.

'I thought if I made an interactive game that explains how things unravelled it might garner some attention to a conflict that I am concerned is being forgotten,' he says. 'Perhaps this will be a way for people that wouldn't be interested to engage with the conflict. If *1,000 Days of Syria* can at least inform and perhaps moti-vate an otherwise naive few, the game will have been a success.'

Navid Khonsari, a forty-four-year-old Iranian developer, is no stranger to seeing his video games garner the kind of attention Swenson was aiming for. Between 2001 and 2005, he worked at Rockstar Games and was a director of production on a number of titles in the *Grand Theft Auto* series, a perennial bedfellow to controversy. But Khonsari's latest project has attracted a differ-ent kind of opprobrium: he has been branded a US spy by the newspapers in Iran, an accusation that prevents him from safely returning to the country he fled thirty-four years ago.

'The Iranian revolution of 1979 is a defining story for me,' Khonsari tells me, 'and it's a story that I keep coming back to.' Khonsari left Rockstar to focus on documentary scripts that he was writing in his spare time, but after founding a development studio with his wife in 2010, he began to look for a different kind of subject for a game. 'With the continuing tensions between the West and Iran, and the Arab Spring, the time was right to highlight the universal themes of revolution.'

Khonsari's game, simply titled *1979 Revolution*, follows a character named Reza, a young photojournalist living in Tehran during the tumultuous days of the Iranian revolution, when the US-supported Pahlavi dynasty was overthrown and replaced with an Islamic republic. While Reza isn't politically or religiously motivated, he is inspired by the idea of change, and incensed by the brutal death of his cousin. He joins the revolution and eventually becomes a key player in its success. The game's plot extends through the hostage crisis and into the violent and uneasy early days of the new regime, when Reza is betrayed by both the revolution and his best friend.

Eschewing the first-person-shooter template for a more interactive adventure-game format, *1979 Revolution* lets players explore Tehran and complete mini-games, their choices shaping the story as it progresses. While sabotaging power grids and hurling rocks at police is a departure from the shooting and carjacking of *Grand Theft Auto*, Khonsari views his games as more alike than not. 'In *1979 Revolution*, like *Grand Theft Auto* and *Max Payne* [a video-game representation of the noir films of the 1940s and 1950s], narrative is at the heart of the experience,' he says. 'The main difference is that my game is set in a real place and time – accountable to history.'

While Swenson's game aspires to be a work of contemporary journalism, Khonsari's is historical fiction. It's also semi-biographical, in that it's informed by Khonsari's personal experiences living in Tehran in the days leading up to the revolution. His was a childhood filled with cultural juxtapositions: Khonsari's bedroom was plastered with *Star Wars* posters, while his family's apartment building was filled with the ducks, chicken or sheep often presented to his father, a surgeon, as payment for treating patients from a nearby village.

'I remember jumping over bonfires in the streets as we celebrated the Zoroastrian holiday of Chah rshanbe Suri before going back inside to watch the *Donny & Marie* show with my family,' he says.

Khonsari hopes to infuse the game with the emotions he felt on the streets as a young boy, using graphic-novel-esque illustrations, historical photography and stock footage. During the revolution's early days, Khonsari's grandfather took him into the streets to see the demonstrations, so he could witness a pivotal moment in the country's history.

'The streets were filled with people and soldiers; helicopters flew overhead as military vehicles roared down major boulevards,' he recalls. 'I felt like I was in a movie.' To recreate those scenes, Khonsari has collaborated with Michel Setboun, a French photojournalist who documented both sides of the revolution. As Reza, players can take photographs in the game and compare their images with the ones taken by Setboun.

Not all of Khonsari's memories are of the vivid spectacle of military power. When Ayatollah Ruhollah Khomeini arrived in Iran, Khonsari and his classmates were instructed to tear pictures of the previous regime's Shah out of their textbooks, and set them on fire. 'All the girls in our class were separated from the boys, and the women in our family had to start covering their hair,' he recalled. Fearing their sons would be drafted into the army, Khonsari's parents decided to flee the country.

Khonsari's father spent three months formulating an escape plan. It was a secret even from the family's closest friends.

'If the new regime found out we planned to defect, we could be in danger, or we could incriminate those members of our family who stayed behind,' Khonsari explains.

Guards began to visit the house to interrogate his father about recent business trips and ask questions about the family's political allegiances. Khonsari's mother prepared a story for her sons to recount in these situations, when the boys were taken into a separate room for questioning.

'It was an awesome responsibility at any age, particularly at that one,' Khonsari says.

Finally, on 22 December 1979, the family left for the airport, claiming to be visiting Canada for a holiday. Khonsari's mother hung as much jewellery around her son's neck and under his shirt as she could.

'I wore an entire lifetime of her jewellery during our flight to Canada,' he recalls.

The memories remain vivid and, for Khonsari, a video game is an ideal way to recreate them in a way that can be shared with others.

As a young teenager in the suburbs of Ontario, Khonsari quickly adapted to his adopted country, immersing himself in the culture – movies, music and video games such as *Donkey Kong* and *Pitfall* – even as his family continued to celebrate Persian rituals.

Khonsari's multicultural identity is reflected in the game, with its Iranian subject matter and Western execution. Asked whether he's making the game for a Western or an Iranian audience, Khonsari says, 'We want to engage everyone, regardless of race, gender or age.'

Like Swenson, Khonsari believes that an international audience will respond to the difficult subject matter precisely because it is a video game.

'Players can engage in a more truthful, raw, political and mature content,' he says. 'We want to go beyond the cinematic storytelling that the film *Argo* started and bring a new level of understanding to this influential time period.' (The game stars Farshad Farahat, who appeared in the Oscar-winning film as a member of the Iranian Revolutionary Guard.)

While the controversy has no doubt increased awareness of the game, the exposure has come at a cost. According to Khonsari, the game's concept artist was forced to flee Iran owing to his association with the project, while many other members of the development team will be left off the game's credits to protect their safety. Are these risks worthwhile?

'In the end, if we can entertain while passively educate,' Khonsari says, 'then yes, we will have accomplished our goals.'

Empathy is usually the reward for vulnerability. When a person invites others into the landscape of their experience with honesty and generosity, most humans respond with kindness and understanding. But not everyone who has attempted to use a video game to tell their own story has been met with this reaction.

In the autumn of 2014 an anonymous message was posted to the discussion-board website 4chan. In it, the author threatened to hurt the video-game developer Zoe Quinn.

'Next time she shows up at a conference we . . . give her a crippling injury that's never going to fully heal . . . a good solid injury to the knees,' it read. 'I'd say a brain damage, but we don't want to make it so she ends up too retarded to fear us.'

For eighteen months prior to this message, the twenty-seven-year-old Quinn received a cavalcade of similar threats, which have created an ambient hum of menace in her life, albeit one that she has mostly been able to ignore. But at the end of August she was doxed, a slang term for document tracing, which is when a person's personal details – home address, phone numbers, bank details and, in some cases, social security number – are made public on the internet. Doxing carries with it an implicit invitation to harangue and harass the subject. After the developer was doxed, the prank calls, threatening e-mails and abusive tweets intensified to such a degree that Quinn, fearing for her safety, chose to leave her home and sleep on friends' sofas.

The reason Quinn was targeted varies, depending on whom you ask, but most explanations lead to *Depression Quest*, a free interactive fiction game released in 2013. To date, it has been played more than a million times. The game, created by Quinn, the writer Patrick Lindsey and the musician Isaac Schankler, casts its player as a young adult suffering from depression. The story is told through snippets of text (which, combined, total forty thousand words), bookended with ostensibly straightforward decisions for the player (it is structurally similar to Swenson's *1,000 Days of Syria*). Will you work at your desk or retreat to bed? Will you attend the party or remain at home? The choices appear mundane, but the protagonist, slowed by depression's fug, finds each one to be tremendously burdensome. For example, some options, such as choosing to 'enthusiastically socialize' at a party, are greyed out, forcing the player's hand.

The hate mail began to arrive on 'pretty much the same day' as the game's release, Quinn tells me. The harassment increased when, earlier this summer, the game launched on Steam, a global digital store for PC games. Many Steam users argued that a game with such a gloomy subject had no place being distributed in the marketplace. Incredulous and angry user reviews filled up *Depression Quest*'s listing page. 'I can't really call it a game since I don't think the point is to entertain you,' reads one. 'I'm not even sure what to say about this thing. It's just boring and is entirely all reading,' says another.

The game debuted on Steam on the day that the news of the actor and comedian Robin Williams's suicide broke, and some critics claimed that the timing of the release was an attempt to capitalise on Williams's death – despite the fact that the game's only source of revenue is donations. Ultimately, Quinn decided to go ahead with the release, because, as she wrote in a blog post, 'I can't in good conscience hold back offering someone something that could help them start making real changes in their life for the sake of reducing the risk of offending people or hurting my own reputation.'

Depression Quest is, like *Revolution 1979*, an autobiographical work. Quinn, who grew up in a small town in the Adirondack mountains in upstate New York, has suffered from depression since she was a teenager. At the age of twelve, she attempted to commit suicide.

'We couldn't afford therapy, so I was sent to meet school-district officials who were less than understanding about teens with depression and suicide issues,' she says. 'I was diagnosed with depression at fourteen, but I couldn't find any medication that did anything for me other than making things worse.'

Video games became Quinn's refuge when her father, a motorbike mechanic, was given a computer by one of his customers as payment. A particular favourite was *Commander Keen*, a game that features an eight-year-old boy who builds a spaceship from household objects and tours the galaxy as earth's defender.

After a break-up, at the age of twenty-four, Quinn moved to Canada.

'My social anxiety was as bad as it had ever been, and now I was in a new country on my own,' she says. 'I was trying to force myself to leave the house and actually interact with people in spite of it.'

Then Quinn saw an advertisement for a six-week course on how to make a video game. 'I figured that maybe it would be a good way to meet people with similar interests,' she says. Six weeks later, she completed her first game. 'I felt like I'd found my calling,' she says.

Game-making provided Quinn with a community and introduced her to Lindsey, who also suffers from depression. Recognising the capacity the medium has for communicating human experience, as Swenson and Khonsari had, Lindsey suggested that the pair attempt to communicate their experiences through a computer game.

'Previous games that attempted to deal with depression or mental illness were too oblique and steeped in metaphor and symbolism to really get at the nasty heart of what living with these conditions can be like,' Lindsey says. 'It is more than "feeling sad". We wanted to communicate what it's like to be in that headspace.'

For Quinn, who also suffers from ADHD, a video game was an ideal way to create an experience that built an understanding between sufferers and non-sufferers. 'Externalising that into a game and asking people to take some time out to see what "rules" other people have to live with, I think, is a powerful use of the medium,' she says.

Depression Quest eschews the usual characteristics of most video games: there is no victorious ending and, as the developers warn in the preamble text, the game 'is not meant to be a fun or light-hearted experience'. It is, instead, one of a growing number of video games that hopes to broaden the medium's subject matter with depictions of life's darker aspects, including titles such as *That Dragon, Cancer*, which documents a family's traumatic experience living with a child suffering from terminal illness, and *Hush*, in which you play a displaced Darfuri child trying to retrieve water while avoiding Janjaweed militia patrols.

This group of games shares few similarities with Mario's spatial-reasoning puzzles and *Call of Duty*'s shooting-gallery tests of reaction speed, typical attributes of the video games that dominate the medium. Some of the hatred directed at Quinn has come from video-game enthusiasts who think that the darker themes are not suitable for video games, which they believe should be playful and primarily focused on entertainment. Others, especially those who have led the recent attacks, claim that the game has received an amount of coverage that is disproportionate to its quality. One criticism is that the game offers too simplistic a solution to depression – it leads the player to partly solve the issue through medication or therapy. But the game explicitly states that it is not trying to speak for all depression sufferers.

'The topic is too big, there's too many people who live with it, and too many moving pieces for anyone to do a definitive statement on what depression is like for everyone,' Quinn says. '*Depression Quest*'s goal was to be a basic introduction to the concept and to get the conversation started.'

Still, some critics argue that the game tells too individual a story, that its protagonist is over-privileged and, therefore, better equipped to deal with the illness than real-world sufferers. Quinn disagrees.

'I deliberately created a protagonist who has a lot of support networks and resources that I don't have,' she says. 'We wanted to pre-empt the argument that someone is only depressed because they have a difficult life. Anyone can have depression. The illness doesn't care how much you do or don't have.'

Not all of the responses to Quinn's game have been so negative. 'I receive many e-mails from players telling me they are thankful that someone out there understands,' she says. '*Depression Quest*'s tone is one of hope. Many players have told me they've tried to take steps in their life to get their illness under control. I tear up while reading my e-mail on subways a lot.' Some therapists have even used the game as an exercise to generate empathy between a sufferer and his or her family, Quinn says.

Though Quinn continues to live with the psychological effects of the dox and the ongoing harassment she's received (people continue to e-mail her daily to say that depression is not a real illness, or, at least, not one that a woman can experience), her belief in being understanding and empathetic remains undiminished.

'They're clearly hurting,' she tells me.

Innocents caught in the crossfire of civil war, parents living with a terminally ill baby, depression sufferers: these are people with whom we naturally empathise. But what of those human beings who are less endearing, whose actions or beliefs we find revolting, rather than engaging? *Super Columbine Massacre RPG*, which attempted to generate empathy with a pair of high-school killers, was, for many, flawed in its execution (too flippant, too cutesy, too unrigorous). But others deny that any such project should have been undertaken, a point of view that, perhaps, springs from the fear that empathising with monsters undermines our ability to feel outrage and scorn.

It is a problem familiar to at least one international terrorist organisation.

In September 2006 al-Qaeda became a game developer.

The organisation's first game release was dubbed *Night of Bush Capturing*, a game free to anyone with an internet connection and an open mind. Its six-mission campaign is constructed from genre features familiar to any follower of video games: work your way deep into enemy territory, shoot enemy soldiers before they shoot you, assassinate the leader (in video-game parlance, the 'final boss'). Only in this case the territory is America, the enemy soldiers are US troops and the leader in question is George W. Bush.

Programmed by a team from al-Qaeda's Global Islamic Media Front, *Night of Bush Capturing* is a modified version of an older, US-made game, *Quest for Saddam*, a game released by Petrilla Entertainment in 2003. *Quest for Saddam* was created by Jesse Petrilla, founder of the United American Committee, a (now defunct) supposedly non-partisan organisation set up to confront Islamic extremism. Al-Qaeda's programmers swapped out the artwork and textures of this earlier game, replacing the crude representations of Arab soldiers and anti-Islamic propaganda with equally crude versions of American soldiers and anti-American propaganda. This straightforward re-skin turned what was intended to be a rallying, pro-Iraq war game into a diametrically opposed, symmetrical attack on George Bush, his foreign policy and the nation behind his presidency.

Neither the original game nor al-Qaeda's transgressive remake was intended to generate empathy. Instead they act as a way for two sides in an ideological conflict to fantasise about domination of the other. There is nothing here, or for that matter in the majority of blockbuster military-themed games that dominate the sales charts, that creates much empathy and understanding – not least because the protagonists are routinely super-heroic soldiers, able to overcome comically insurmountable odds. There is no vulnerability here to invite compassion or identification. Nevertheless, both games found themselves at the forefront of a global debate on freedom of speech, artistic expression and the importance of story and setting in video games.

Wafaa Bilal is an Iraqi–American artist and an associate arts professor at New York University's Tisch School of the Arts, known internationally for his online performative and interactive works that aim to provoke dialogue about international politics. In 2008 Bilal created a version of al-Qaeda's *Night of Bush Capturing* in which he integrates himself into the game's narrative to present his own commentary on the conflict. He renamed the game *Virtual Jihadi* before presenting it to the world as a piece to challenge viewers and inspire debate and conversation.

Bilal's twenty-one-year-old brother, an Iraqi citizen, was killed by shrapnel during a firefight in Najaf. In the game Bilal casts himself as a suicide bomber who, after learning of the real-life death of his brother in the war, is recruited by al-Qaeda to join the hunt for the US president, George Bush. Through his work Bilal says that he intends to 'bring attention to the vulnerability of Iraqi civilians, highlight racist generalisations and stereotypes promoted in video games, and demonstrate how British and American foreign policy is pushing Iraqi citizens into the arms of violent groups like al-Qaeda'.

It's a bold and broad purpose and one that saw Bilal invited by the Rensselaer Polytechnic Institute to present a lecture and exhibit on this work in February 2008. But the exhibition was open for only an hour before city officials shut it down. According to newspaper reports, the decision came after the college Republicans called the arts department 'a safe haven for terrorists'.

'While I'm not a big gamer, I realise that games are now a huge part of our lives,' Bilal tells me. 'Video games are moving from being reactive to more dynamic and interactive. For a long time we did not have interactive mediums but only reactive ones. I think that video games can be more effective and powerful than other mediums such as film in conveying a message, in part because they are an active experience that allows the participant to create the narrative. Video games are the medium of our time.'

As *Quest for Saddam* and *Night of Bush Capturing* were already out there, modifying these controversial examples added weight to my message.'

Bilal is unequivocal about the nature of that message.

'I am trying to engage people in a conversation,' he says. 'We, in the United States of America, have become isolated in a comfort zone. We are so far removed from the conflict. In a way I wanted to hold a mirror to people's faces to let them see the reality of this war's repercussions and explore the fallacy in our culture's denial of that disconnection and their stereotyping of other cultures. In a sense I want to reverse the role of the hunter and the hunted.'

Bilal, in other words, intends to generate empathy through role reversal.

'The original game, *Quest for Saddam*, did not get any attention from the media and the State Department because the ideas it promoted – that all Muslims are terrorists – was the norm. Then, when the game was modified to become the *Night of Bush Capturing*, the State Department labelled the game as a piece of terrorist propaganda and a recruitment tool. I thought that was strange because the only thing al-Qaeda did is to replace the Iraqi skins with American soldiers' skins and Saddam's skin with Bush's skin. What exactly made it propaganda where it wasn't before?

'My game reverses the roles, viewing the conflict seen in countless first-person shooters from the other side. And people in the US do not like what they see – or rather, what they heard, since the game was open for less than one hour before it was closed down. This reaction reinforces my belief that a "superior" culture will always impose its point of view on the rest of the world. And when someone speaks out effectively, he or she gets labelled. That is a sign of culture in trouble because it cannot accept a different point of view.'

The opportunity that video games present to an individual to experience different roles and situations to those available to us in daily life is part of their great appeal (and perhaps a part of what makes them all-consuming: there's always another way of life to try out in these virtual dimensions when you tire of your own). Usually games act as surrogates for activities that are too expensive, demanding, dangerous or time-consuming. But in the hands of the right designer, this same power can be used to create a different kind of insight.

While experiencing life from another person's perspective can be challenging (it may, for example, generate empathy towards a person or situation that you would prefer to remain distanced from), it is also deeply fascinating. Humans are irrepressibly interested in other people's lives (the soaps, the docudramas, the gossip magazines). Games offer a new way to satisfy our curiosity, one that has an entirely different texture and immediacy to television or print. And video games are not only a way for an audience to experience a life outside of their own, but also a powerful way for a person to invite others into their own personal history and perspective, to not only view the story from the sidelines, but from the inside. And in becoming a soldier, an oil baron, a city planner, a disenfranchised terrorist, a teenager suffering from mental-health issues, a displaced Syrian child, we begin to understand the world and the other people who inhabit it a little more.

08

HIDING
PLACE

Chris Ferguson had almost given up on video games when he first visited *Skyrim*.

'The power fantasies had worn me out,' he tells me. 'Whether it was pretending to be the perfect sportsman or a man changing the world through the power of guns, I was bored of the fantasy. As I began to adjust to the idea of fatherhood, I was more or less ready to leave all that behind.'

Ferguson and his wife, Sarah, had been married for seven years and, during that time, had 'never not been trying for a baby'. In that sense, the news that the pair was expecting a baby wasn't unexpected, but it was still a surprise.

Like many who hear the news for the first time in their lives, the pair began to try on the idea of being parents. They bought a red and blue Babygro that said 'Just Like Daddy' across the chest and a pair of those implausibly tiny infant socks. They celebrated their final Christmas as two.

On New Year's Day, Sarah was taken to hospital, where she underwent an operation to remove the ectopic pregnancy that threatened her life. This is caused when a fertilised egg implants itself outside of the womb, usually in one of the fallopian tubes. Stuck in this tubular limbo, the egg is unable to grow into a baby. Around one in every hundred pregnancies is ectopic. If caught early enough, it's treatable with few side effects. If left undetected, it can cause the tube to rupture, causing life-threatening internal bleeding and often resulting in the loss of one of the woman's fallopian tubes. Sarah's tube had ruptured.

'It felt like a miracle to get pregnant at all, and then to have that taken away . . .' Ferguson says. 'But it was never a viable pregnancy at all. That's a funny thing to have to get over. Because in your head it's been your baby, but in truth it was never something that had a chance to become a baby. You then have to come to terms with the fact that it might have been your only chance to have a baby. The human body does make some allowances for only having one fallopian tube, but it was still devastating.'

After the operation Ferguson wasn't allowed into the ward to see Sarah, who needed rest. In the chaos of the emergency, no one had taken a moment to explain to him why, as he puts it, he wasn't going to be a dad any longer. Instead, they sent him home.

'I couldn't sleep,' he says. 'There was no question of me going to sleep. I was dazed. I'm not someone who can sit and watch a film. I have the patience to read a book or refresh Twitter all day, but I can't watch a film. But video games . . . I can do that.'

Ferguson had been given a video game for Christmas. He put the disc into the drive and began to play.

Skyrim is the name of a vast region set in the northern part of the fictional land of Tamriel after which the game, launched in 2011, is named. It's a hardy, unforgiving place, home to the Nords, a people toughened by decades spent battling frost. Lines of coniferous trees, defiant and snow-dusted, surround its ice lakes. Grey mountains rise and fall in the distance, clouds draped around their necks. The wind whips up angrily, lifting with it white, swirling powder.

It is a world shared by beasts both mythical and real. Elk canter. Rabbits bound, then lift quivering noses to sniff for threats before returning to the whisper and scurry of their busy work. Clicking, overgrown crabs patrol the shoreline. Woolly mammoths tread heavily through the snow. At night you're just as likely to run into a cruel giant as a fox. Freeze the frame and you have a picture postcard: Iceland with the contrast turned up. Dig a little deeper and you find Iceland with a cave-troll infestation. There are friends to be made here, in the nooks and valleys, but generally Skyrim regards you as an unwanted visitor: the land and its people try to expel you.

This place of virtual cold and grim scarcity is not a typical refuge.

In *Skyrim* you can choose to bring peace or turmoil to the land. The native Nord race want to free their land from Imperial interference, to become independent. The Imperial Legion, the military of the Empire, seeks instead to reunite and pacify the province. To a certain degree, you are free to choose with whom to side.

One of Ferguson's frustrations with video games at the time was his own tendency to race towards the goal, rather than take time to explore and enjoy the journey.

'Something that I've learned about myself is that, if a game's story is based on saving the world, I will concentrate all of my attention on that goal,' he says. 'Other characters in the game might implore me to carry out side-quests, helping them with this and that, but I usually never engage in that because . . . well, because the world needs saving and that seems more important.'

This time, however, was different. Ferguson spent his time roaming *Skyrim*'s world, wandering and, as he puts it, exploring for exploration's sake. For Ferguson, this freedom to set his pace and manage his destiny was key to being able to escape the turmoil in his mind and in his home.

'If it had been a shooter or something, I'm not sure I would have fallen into it in the same way,' he says. 'It's not constantly intense. There's room to wander. It also gets the power fantasy thing right. You have power to change things while none of the missions you're given are particularly taxing.'

A few days later Sarah returned home.

'I remember when I took her back from the hospital I was scared that I'd never bring her back to life,' says Ferguson. 'She was empty and broken. I brought her tea and beans on toast and when she slept I played. Sometimes, when the loading screens went on too long, I'd start crying. She would call to me and I would pause the game and go and sit with her and tell her that the important thing was that she was well and safe and that she would get better.'

Ferguson gathered up the vials of folic acid, the baby books and the red and blue Babygro, placed the items in a plastic bag and hid it in a drawer.

'I didn't want her to see any of it,' he says.

Sometimes visitors would visit and Ferguson would make them tea.

'We'd sit and they would leave their coats on. Everyone had such serious faces.'

Sarah remained in bed for a week. She needed drugs every four hours, which Ferguson administered. He spent the rest of the time cooking, cleaning or retreating into *Skryim*.

'I flitted between these few rooms, these two realities,' he recalls.

Entertainment, particularly the sort that can be consumed from the comfort of a chair, often has a utilitarian role in our lives. People might chain-watch soap operas as a way to steady their emotions in the wake of a break-up, or revert to cartoons with easily digestible messages and morals when the complexities of life's decisions weigh too heavily.

With video games, the effect is different. In the modernised Netflix adaptation of the BBC television series *House of Cards*, Kevin Spacey's character, a high-flying American politician, is shown playing online competitive video games as a way to unwind and destress from the wrangling and machinations of his political life at the end of each day. Many share Frank Underwood's habit: video games serve a specific purpose in the day's schedule, a way to escape from the rigours of the preceding hours in a virtual space or, perhaps, in some way to make sense of them. What makes them unique is that these are places where one's actions and decisions do not have to be so carefully weighed: outcomes are usually predictable, reliable and, if necessary, easily undone.

If, while playing *SimCity*, you decide to place a new sewerage treatment works near a residential district and upset the citizens who you, as mayor, are supposed to be looking out for, you can simply turn back the clock to an earlier save to undo their anger. Such mistakes are indelible in real life. In *Braid*, a game that gives its player control over time itself, every mistimed jump can be un-jumped with a squeeze of a button, every action rehearsed and repeated till it is perfected.

Then there are the games that provide a more numbing kind of escapism. Descend into Hyrule, the setting for each of Shigeru Miyamoto's Zelda games, and there's no need for the high-stakes precision of a *Braid* or *SimCity*. This is, rather, a place to which you acclimatise then swill about in, pursuing goals often of your own choosing, at your own tempo.

This kind of scrappy catharsis is beautifully presented in a dif-ferent way by *Katamari Damacy*, a Japanese game in which you must roll an adhesive ball around a series of domestic locations, rolling up household detritus (till the ball grows large enough to be fired into space). There's something deeply liberating about the act of decluttering the modern world (as the sticky ball grows larger you're able to exit into the surrounding Tokyo streets, rolling up cars and bus stops, benches and ice-cream vans), a feeling that reflects the sense of peaceful clarity we can feel after tidying a desk, clearing out a spare room or making our lives less complicated.

For Ferguson, bewildered with grief and confusion, Skyrim was a place he was able to visit in order to be anchored. It might seem strange that a human might choose to find their feet in a place that doesn't exist. But when reality has let you down with an event of colossal indifference and capriciousness, the reliable rules and outcomes of a video game become all the more inviting.

Skyrim may not have been a sacred space for Ferguson, but looking back at that time today, he does believe that the game gave him a specific type of escapism that, in the moment, he needed.

'It is a game that rewards you for doing the same things over and over again, allowing you to get better at them, refining your skills by constant iteration,' he says. 'I was in a cold, mechanical world where I was getting better, getting powerful.'

Perhaps it was the comfort of feeling that he was in control of his own destiny again, after an event that showed with such clarity how there are some things in life that no man can control. But whatever comfort the game gave him, it was complicated by guilt.

'There was part of me that thought I was doing the wrong thing,' he says. 'I'm not sure what else I should have been doing, but I felt guilty about spending all of this time within the game. It was a real opportunity to disappear into another world, and I was never entirely comfortable with how readily I embraced that.'

Eventually, his wife Sarah left her bed. She would watch her husband play for a while. 'At a certain point there were bigger emotional problems for us to deal with, but for a while, it was enough to sit there together, visiting this cold place.'

While Ferguson appeared quietly resilient to his visitors, his internal feelings were different. 'We weren't sad and brave,' he says. 'We were angry. But I don't think that came through in the way that I played the game. I played through in quite a law-abiding way. I chose to be moral. Even in the combat I snuck around. If my character had reflected the way that I was I would have bought a giant broadsword and attacked everything in sight.'

Then one day, a few weeks after he started his journey in *Skyrim*, Ferguson was finished.

'When Sarah started to recover that's when I started to become emotional for the first time,' he says. 'I stopped playing the game. I had a realisation that this just wasn't where I wanted to be any more.'

There was ceremony to the break-up. Ferguson removed the disc from its tray, opened up a menu on the console and began to delete his save games – those digital files that record a player's progress in the game – one by one. *Skyrim* saves a player's progress in an unusual way, creating a new file every few minutes, a breadcrumb trail of historical record. By the end of an adventure that can last for scores of hours, there are often hundreds of files.

'Looking at all those saves was upsetting to me,' he says. 'There's a part of your brain that believes playing a game in tragic circumstances is stolen time, that should have been spent doing something else. To see hundreds of those saves laid out confronted me. I remember I was telling myself that I needed space on my hard drive. But I never download anything, so I absolutely didn't need to do it for that reason. I had done everything I could do in the game, or at least everything that I was interested in doing. So I guess there was a sense of closure there. The save files were a record that I was embarrassed about. It was time that I'd put into a virtual life, rather than a real one. There was guilt. Eradicating the saves was perhaps a way to get rid of that feeling. Or maybe just a way of saying goodbye to that time altogether.'

A few weeks later Ferguson was able to say goodbye to the time spent in the game in a more definitive way when a friend visited.

'He mentioned that he wanted to play *Skyrim* but couldn't afford a copy,' he recalls. 'So I gave him mine. It felt good to have something to give that someone wanted. But there was something else, I guess. A sense of closure.'

It's clear to me why Ferguson found solace in a video game at that time: it gave him something to do, a series of easily digestible tasks which he could complete without needing to leave his wife's side and, as a result, a sense of progress and movement when the rest of his life's plans had been obliterated. I remember when, as a teenager, my parents first separated. I too found routine and direction in a video game (mine was *Final Fantasy VII*) when the framework of my life seemed to be collapsing.

Literature is able to remove us from our own lives and focus on the hopes, dreams and conflicts of another. But only a video game gives us the sense of being in control, of being the author of our destiny.

Strangely, it's for this precise reason that Ferguson, who now works for Edinburgh University and has a young son, is reluctant to recommend video games as a salve for the wounded soul.

'It can be a problem to get lost in fiction – and I include films and children's literature in this – that's centred around manifest destiny and the idea that everyone is a good guy or a bad guy. These kinds of stories are useful for certain stages in a human being's development, but it's not how the world works. It's simplistic and sometimes we can cling on to these stories that were supposed to be for childhood into adulthood. In games it seems unhealthy to me that you usually play as the hero who can overcome all odds, and who must destroy anyone who stands in opposition or disagreement.'

Despite the reservations, Ferguson recognises the role that *Skyrim* played, if not in his healing, then in his survival at the time.

'If you play games because you just need a break from the real world then, with that caveat, I do believe that it can be helpful. Games can provide respites from the storms of the real world. People do that with all kinds of fiction. For Sarah, it was watching hundreds of episodes of *Gilmore Girls*. It's the consumption of something that is reassuring, something that displays shades of the real world, but that is also a simplified, comforting version, which has aspects that you can control in some way. It makes sense that this would be something people retreat into when life feels out of control.'

A few months after I first heard Ferguson's story, I visited Tale of Tales, a two-person independent game developer based in Ghent, Belgium. The pair, a husband-and-wife team, make art games that bear little resemblance to *Skyrim* or the other blockbuster titles that reach the billboards and advertising hoardings.

After I arrived they took me into the city, where the spires of St Bavo's Cathedral prod at the Belgian sky, which was, on this particular day, a uniform September grey. Inside the building a Gothic warren of chambers and alcoves was warm with bodies and candlelight, a refuge from the post-summer downer that is September outside.

'The problem with God being dead is that nobody builds cathedrals any more,' Auriea Harvey said. 'And humans *need* cathedrals.

Or, at very least, they need somewhere to go for refuge, reflection, sanctuary and rest.'

While Harvey and her husband, Michaël Samyn, are not religious in any formal sense, they come here often, she told me. Sometimes they visit in order to revisit the dominant aesthetic of Samyn's adolescence – he attended Catholic school, with all of its attendant ritual, art and arcana. Sometimes they come to be inspired, not by the aesthetic but by the *utility*.

'I think that, at their best, video games are able to perform something of the cathedral's function in the modern world,' she says. 'At least, that's my hope for the games that we make, that they might be sacred spaces in some way.'

This has been my own experience of the pair's work, their numerous 'cathedrals of fire', which bear almost no similarities with the violence and noise of the mainstream video-game industry's more familiar and routine output. In 2005's *The Endless Forest*, for example, an online game commissioned by the Musée d'Art Moderne Grand-Duc Jean in Luxembourg, you play as a rangy deer that interacts with other players, each of whom also plays as a deer, through sound and movement. Some of the attributes of the vast online game worlds such as *World of Warcraft* are seen here, such as the ability to customise characters' appearance with new antlers, pelts and adorning flowers in order to personalise the game and show off to others. But there are no enemies to vanquish, and, in most cases, you are only able to change the appearance of other deer. If you want to change your own appearance, you must find a way to enlist another player's help, convincing them to cast a spell on you that, for example, grants you red antlers, or pink eyes. You can hop, trot, make sounds and even dance with other deer, but there is no chat-box to allow for open communication. In this way, *The Endless Forest* is an ephemeral tribute to primal communication that demonstrates the value of the unspoken in online games. More broadly, it's an ode to the mystic gloom found beneath a canopy of trees and, as per Harvey's hope, a virtual place to revitalise the soul.

The Graveyard, another of Tale of Tales' works that was nominated for the Innovation Award in the Independent Games Festival in 2009, is more peaceful still. In this game – or rather place – you're cast as an elderly woman with a walking stick who trudges between phalanxes of gravestones en route to a bench. Presented in noirish black and white and soundtracked by yapping crows, distant sirens and the crunch of the gravel underfoot, it's a quietly subversive work. The understated experience lasts for just ten minutes, unusual in a medium that prizes length and expanse. Tale of Tales made the game free, but for five dollars players can purchase a premium version that adds just one feature: the possibility that the woman will die during the sequence. It's a quiet reflection on age, death and remembrance.

These games have been created specifically to perform a utilitarian function in the player's life, be that as a space to interact with others without troublesome social mores, or the pressure of having to create scintillating conversation, or as a space to find peace, and to reflect on our own histories.

But in some parts of the world, video games are not only psychological or spiritual places of refuge. In certain contexts, the hiding place isn't metaphorical.

Yousif Mohammed is only nineteen, but he is one of the world's top players in the online video game *Battlefield 3*. A realistic military first-person shooter that sold more than eight million copies in the months following its release in 2011, it no doubt feels closer to home for Mohammed than for the Western players it was primarily designed for – one of its missions, dubbed Operation

Swordbreaker, is set within Mohammed's adopted home city of Sulaymaniyah.

During the past two decades, life for many Iraqis has been turbulent and perilous. In 2006, while Baghdad was still experiencing the war's aftermath, ten-year-old Mohammed was playing in a park in the city with a friend when he saw a man in a parked car lean out of the window and stare at them through a camcorder's viewfinder. Believing that he would appear on television that night, Mohammed hurried home to tell his parents what he'd seen. His mother, Amna Mohammed, an engineer in the Iraqi Ministry of Water Resources, didn't believe her son until, later that evening, she received a phone call from the mother of Mohammed's friend, confirming what had happened.

'At that time, there was a gang operating in the area that kidnapped kids and demanded money for their release – around fifty thousand dollars,' she told me.

The gang operated in the Mansour district, a relatively wealthy neighbourhood in western Baghdad, where the family lived. Typically, the gang released the children after receiving the ransom money, but, in one notorious incident, they killed the hostage even after receiving payment.

Amna knew that boys like Mohammed were prime targets, so she sent him and his grandmother away from Baghdad later that night. The pair took a six-hour taxi ride to Kurdistan before heading into the northern city of Sulaymaniyah.

'Any mother, believing that their child was in grave danger, would have done what I did,' she told me. Amna stayed behind with her husband to settle the family's affairs before joining her son. The escape had a profound effect on Mohammed: he left in such haste that he didn't pack any of his toys, including, most distressingly, his video-game console. Alone in a new city, with no friends, the boy felt grimly isolated.

'Gaming had been a big part of my daily activities, so when I fled to this city, I was at a loss,' he said. 'After a few months, I bought a computer again and, through that, met other players and began to feel settled.'

Today, Mohammed is an aspiring doctor, as well as one of the country's top video-game players. After his family resettled, he threw himself into gaming, both as a means of escape and to make new friends. He excels at the latest blockbuster American titles, particularly first-person shooters like *Battlefield 3*, a game that he has spent seven hundred and twenty-one hours playing. He is currently ranked in the top two per cent of players in the world.

His parents' generation views his hobby with some distrust: like many Western parents, they worry about shooting games and the possibility that they could encourage violence. But, for the most part, Mohammed's parents supported the hobby, because it kept him inside and safe. For the same reason, many Iraqi children are encouraged to play as much as they like, because the country remains volatile. Video games have become a way to keep a generation away from the capricious bombings that have made the streets some of the most perilous in the world. They are a physical refuge, as well as a psychological one.

'Video games are the only viable entertainment we have here,' says Mohannad Abdulla, a twenty-five-year-old network administrator for Baghdad's main internet service provider. He's been playing games since he was a teenager; a poster of Captain Price, a fictional British Army officer from the video game *Call of Duty*, hangs on his wall. 'Other hobbies are just too dangerous because of terrorism. We don't have clubs, so games are the only way to have some fun with friends and stay safe at home, where there is no risk of being killed by a suicide bomber. For many of us, video games are our only escape from these miseries.'

During Saddam Hussein's rule, it was difficult to buy them, and only relatively well-off, professional-class families like Mohammed's could afford to import titles from Europe. Until the advent of disc-based video games in the mid-nineties, it was too difficult to pirate game cartridges.

'The industry is still in its infancy in Iraq,' says Omar M. Alanseri, the owner of the Iraqi Games Centre, one of only a small number of dedicated video-game retailers in Baghdad, which opened sixteen months ago. 'But each year, more people get involved. I've seen the audience vastly increase, especially among teenagers.'

Some of the most popular video games in Iraq, as in America, are military-themed shooters, in which the player assumes the role of a soldier and blasts through waves of virtual enemies.

'Almost all of my friends play video games like *World of Tanks* [and] *Battlefield 3*,' says Abdulla. 'In fact, we have some of the top-ranked players in the world here.'

This interest in military games stems from the local environment as much as, in the case of many Western players, male vanity.

'Growing up, my life was completely military-focused,' Abdulla says. 'It is the way we are raised. For example, I was taught how to use an AK-47 when I was in elementary school. Younger players who are not so affected by Saddam's agendas play other game types more easily than we do, like *Minecraft* and other non-military games.'

Many of these first-person shooters, often created with input from US military advisers – a handful of Navy SEALs were punished for consulting on the 2012 video game *Medal of Honor: Warfighter* – are set against the backdrop of fictionalised real-world conflicts, often within Middle Eastern countries.

Some have entire sections set within Iraq, like the *Battlefield* series.

For Abdulla, playing these games in their real-world settings isn't problematic.

'Any video game that's set within Iraq and involves killing terrorists becomes instantly famous here,' he says. 'Everyone wants to play it. We have been through so much because of terror. Shooting terrorists in a game is cathartic. We can have our revenge in some small way.' Alanseri agrees: 'Any game that has a level set in Iraq is popular. They always sell more copies than other games because they are related in some way to our lives.' The games have even established a kind of empathy for foreign gaming partners that Alanseri said he would not otherwise have. 'I have learned a lot of things, like Western-world values, culture, lifestyle, and even the way that they think through video games.'

Mohammed believes that the friendships he has formed through online gaming have had a transformative effect on the way in which some people view his country.

'Some people told me they were scared of Iraqis,' he says, 'thinking that they are all terrorists. But in reality, we are victims. When they got to know me, they saw the truth and changed their minds about Iraqis. It removed the fear.'

A twenty-two-year-old Norwegian, Michael Moe, is now one of Mohammed's closest friends. The young men met online while playing *Battlefield 3*, and now speak on the phone or over Skype every few days.

'I become worried about Mohammed if I do not hear from him for any more than two days,' says Moe. 'I always check up on him when that happens.'

Abdulla almost seems to prefer friends he has made playing online video games.

'Here in our home country, most of us have lost some, if not most, of our friends,' he says. 'They were either killed or fled Iraq. And you can't just trust anyone any more. So a friend across seas who you can trust is better than a friend here who might stab your back any minute.'

Video games will not solve Iraq's ongoing challenges. But for some young Iraqis, they do provide more than a mere distraction from the terrors of life in the country. The social connections that they encourage, both within Iraq and beyond, have built empathy in ways that may have a profound effect on the way some young people view their place in the world.

For Amna, Mohammed's mother, the effect has been less grand and more localised.

'I used to object about video games,' she says. 'I wanted Mohammed to spend more time studying. But I've come to see the strange benefits. Video games have broadened his relationships outside of our borders, and formed new bonds. He loves his gaming friends and, from what I can tell, they love him, too.'

Battlefield's Swedish creators could never have known that their game, based on contemporary urban warfare, would play an active role in keeping one young player away from the risks of genuine urban warfare. There are other pastimes, of course, that could have provided the same function (fifty years ago Mohammed might have had his nose buried n a comic book). But as we've seen, the video game passes the time more efficiently and in a more prolonged manner than most. *Battlefield* in particular offers Mohammed a way to feel in control of his circumstances, just as *Skyrim* offered Ferguson a way to take control of a reality, when the world outside of the game was turbulent and untethered.

In different ways but for similar reasons, Mohammed and

Ferguson's stories illustrate something crucial about the role that video games (*all* games, arguably) fulfil for human beings: a way to step outside of reality for a fleeting moment in order to better understand ourselves and the world in which we live when, at last, we're ready to return.

09

MYSTERY

INSERT COIN TO CONTINUE

Way out in southeastern Flint County, Back o Beyond is the most isolated area in San Andreas. The trees loom conspiratorially. Their branches knit together, as if holding down the gloom. As night falls, a fog rises, muffling the air. For some, it's a place of tranquillity, far away from the noise and fury of the cities nearby. But for others, this forsaken forest is not a place of isolation. Here, they believe, you are never alone.

In 2004, Rob Silver was driving his truck through Back o Beyond when he caught sight of something in the thicket.

'Out of the corner of the television screen I saw a large, tall, dark figure,' he tells me, the memory still alive. 'It happened twice, both times during that first year. To this day, I've not come across the creature again.'

A decade later Kaleb Krimmel, a teenager from Michigan, had a similar experience.

'I have seen strange figures in the fog before, but pedestrians can sometimes appear in weird places,' he says. 'While this sort of computer error describes most of my encounters, this time was different. I was in Back o Beyond, walking up a hill. It was foggy out, but behind some plants I clearly saw a giant black figure. I aimed my camera to take a picture, but by the time I steadied the viewfinder it was gone.'

Silver and Krimmel are not the only players who claim to have seen Bigfoot in the virtual forests of *Grand Theft Auto: San Andreas*, a video game released in 2004 in which players assume the role of a young gang member, Carl Johnson, in a story that draws upon various real-life events in Los Angeles, most centrally the rivalry between the Bloods and Crips street gangs and the simmering tensions of the Rodney King riots. The game, set in 1992 within the fictional state of San Andreas, a geographical amalgam of California and Nevada, sold more than twenty-seven million copies worldwide. If its developers had included a rare occurrence of a Bigfoot character in the Back o Beyond, occasional sightings from the masses of scouring players would be inevitable. Within months of the game's release, videos allegedly showing sightings of Bigfoot appeared on the internet, while viewers debated their authenticity in the comments.

These discussions were muddied when some enterprising fans created a 'mod', an alternative code that can be downloaded and installed, to insert a fabricated Bigfoot into the game, complicating the hunt for the 'real' virtual Bigfoot. Nevertheless, more than a decade after the game's release, a number of communities continue to work to prove the authenticity of Bigfoot's existence in the original game, and devoted users still upload photographs of unusual footprints and other pieces of circumstantial evidence to their websites. Silver runs one such site.

'Many people make the Bigfoot myth out to be some fan-made story that's simply gotten out of hand,' he tells me. 'In fact, the staff at the *Grand Theft Auto* website I contributed to at the time didn't want anything to do with myths, and refused to have them catalogued. Last November, I set out to make the most comprehensive, informative *Grand Theft Auto* myth site on the Web.'

The Bigfoot debate in the game closely mirrors the Bigfoot debate in the real world, in which believers often clash with sceptics. Silver's belief in the creature's existence is absolute.

'I one hundred per cent believe Bigfoot exists within San Andreas,' he says. Krimmel agrees: 'I do believe the creature exists. I have encountered him more than once. I would say he is proven.'

But detractors say the myth's disciples are fooling themselves.

'Either they're mistaken, or they're lying,' says a sceptical forum user. 'Myth hunters are determined to believe in myths despite all evidence to the contrary. Perhaps they want the myths to be true so badly that they've managed to trick themselves into seeing things that aren't there, or they've made connections between things that aren't connected. Maybe they're just lying or stupid, or both.'

One crucial advantage the Bigfoot hunters in the game have over their real-world counterparts is that they're able to communicate with the game's creators. *Grand Theft Auto*'s developer, Rockstar North, has not been silent on the issue. Speaking to an American video-game magazine shortly after the game's release, the game's lead level designer, Craig Filshie, said that there was 'not a bit of truth' to the Bigfoot rumours.

'If you look closely, you'll notice that all of the screenshots are typically retouched versions of screenshots we created for magazines before the game was released,' he said.

Would magazines go so far as to fake such images? And if so, why would they only do so with this game? It's not like we're being inundated with stills that claim to show a blurred chupacabra in *Super Mario*, a Loch Ness monster in *Call of Duty*, a yeti in *Tetris*.

Filshie even went so far as to offer his own explanation for what Bigfoot-sighters might be seeing in the game: 'San Andreas is an extremely complex game, with millions of lines of code,' he said at the time. 'It's entirely possible for strange things to happen, but none of them are intentional.'

Terry Donovan, the CEO of Rockstar, also speaking at the

time, said, 'There is no Bigfoot, just like in real life.'

This straightforward denial from the game's makers should have been enough to quash the rumours – as if God himself had confirmed to the world that there were no hirsute monsters roaming America's tangled forests. But a video game with a scope like *Grand Theft Auto* is a vast and multifaceted construction, built by teams of hundreds of people. It's entirely possible that one artist or designer could have inserted a so-called Easter egg like Bigfoot without the rest of the team's knowledge. Indeed, some coders concealed a sex-based mini-game – which became known as 'hot coffee' – that led to the company being brought in front of the US Federal Trade Commission in 2006. It was a scandal that cost the game's publisher, Take Two, more than twenty million dollars in lawsuit payments. If a fully developed mini-game, which allowed the game's lead character to have graphic sex with women, could be surreptitiously included in the game, it's no great stretch to believe that a single rogue programmer or artist could have quietly inserted a mythical beast.

Virtual Bigfoot sceptics have another advantage over their real-life counterparts: they are able to scour the game's code in search of evidence. If there were no Bigfoot assets (the graphic renderings necessary to represent any object in a game world) it would prove that virtual Bigfoot was a myth. Some motivated sceptics have spent countless hours scanning the code; they claim that, in the thousands upon thousands of lines of programming, there is nothing referring to Bigfoot. But others are dubious of these claims; after all, how meticulous could an amateur, unpaid hacker sleuth really be?

Despite its early denials, Rockstar has only added to the sense of doubt in recent years. When asked to comment on the rumours, a Rockstar spokesperson told me, 'We'd prefer to keep an air of mystery surrounding the topic. Let the myth remain a myth.' Christian Cantamessa, a former Rockstar employee who worked as a level designer on the game, took a similar stance when I approached him.

'It is a little like asking the US government to discuss Area 51, isn't it?' he said. 'The only appropriate comment is "No comment".'

For myth-hunters, the search for Bigfoot has provided an ongoing and compelling reason to continue playing the game long after the main storyline has been exhausted. While Chris Ferguson, the Scottish man who retreated into *Skyrim* in the aftermath of personal tragedy, used the game to seek refuge, an introspective kind of quest, these intrepid hunters visit their game to seek a different kind of answer. Their quest is related to discovery (what will we find?) and to glory (the chance to become the first to bag Bigfoot), but it's centrally about mystery, and, in the tradition of all human investigations, the thrill of finding a solution.

Krimmel visits San Andreas twice a week in search of Bigfoot, taking an in-game camera with him on his excursions in the hope of photographing the creature.

'I've beaten the game twice, and maxed out my stats, so myth-hunting is the only thing left to do,' he says.

For Silver, the allure is in the chance to catch sight of something rare and wonderful: 'There's a one-in-a-hundred shot at finding him, in my opinion. That possibility is why I return.'

Whether or not people are disposed to believe in or disregard legends, the San Andreas Bigfoot myth appears to be self-perpetuating. As newer and younger players gain access to the game and read the online rumours, some are inexorably drawn into the story, and become active participants in its extension. It's a worldwide phenomenon. Rhem Alhatimy, a fourteen-year-old resident of Kufa, Iraq, bought a pirated copy of the game a few months ago, on a DVD containing each of the PC titles in the long-running *Grand Theft Auto* series.

'I'd read the rumours, and decided to visit Back o Beyond myself,' he tells me. 'It was about three o'clock in the morning. That's when I saw it: a dark, creepy thing standing in the woods. I'm not one hundred per cent certain, but I think that was him.

'I will keep looking,' Alhatimy continues. 'There is something in those woods.'

Final Fantasy VII, the Japanese adventure game in which I found refuge during my teenage years, gained notoriety because it kills off one of its main characters midway through the story. This was, at the time, an unprecedented act in video games. Losing a fictional character whom you care about often stings, but in a video game, the characters you control carry more than mere emotional investment. They are also graphical representations of invested effort – these are the avatars into which you have poured your time and energy, which have grown in power and competence thanks to your service and dedication leading them to victory. When Aeris dies in *Final Fantasy VII* the wound is doubly deep: the game's writers are taking away not only a character with whom you identify and about whom you care, but also an asset that you have carefully nurtured in your route to victory.

Even before the game's release in the West in 1997, importers of the Japanese version reported Aeris's death and rumours began to spread that there was a way to bring the character back to life. Complicated sets of instructions for how to resurrect Aeris were disseminated across the emerging internet.

Some of their authors claimed to be members of the development team, or to have tangential links to the game's writers, in order to add weight to their claims. Players around the world invented theories and tried them out, using ever more convoluted methods.

This kind of scrabbling incredulity as a reaction to loss in fiction has precedent. Charles Dickens's *The Old Curiosity Shop* was published in instalments in the author's own weekly periodical, *Master Humphrey's Clock*. Within three days of publishing Chapter 53, in which one lovable character, Little Nell, visits an old church and has a conversation in a graveyard, Dickens had received several letters warning the writer to refrain from what they believed he was planning. These readers took Nell's visit to the graveyard in conjunction with the line that she looked 'pale but very happy' as a foreshadowing of her death.

There's an anecdotal story that, in subsequent weeks, American readers stormed New York City's piers, demanding to know from visitors from England whether or not Nell had died.

Nell does indeed perish and Dickens was swarmed with letters expressing anger and heartbreak. In the realm of fiction, readers have the opportunity to appeal to the character's creator in a bid to have death's sentence reversed. So it was with Aeris, who had petitions started in her name. The game's developer, Squaresoft, reportedly received letters and e-mails either berating their decision or demanding to know how it might be undone.

What was most interesting was the way in which thousands of players hunted for the solution – if the game's authors weren't going to find a way to bring this character back, perhaps they could find a way, some glitch in the programming code from which salvation might be drawn. This was, after all, a game, which came with a clutch of secrets, including characters that could be recruited to the story only by, for example, exploring the depths of the oceans in a submarine.

This sense of mystery, of a character that can be saved, or of a hidden monster that can be tracked and photographed, can prove a powerful draw back into a game whose charms might otherwise have been exhausted. It's something that the earliest game designers trained players to search for, either in the tips pages in the backs of magazines (where secrets were, often, revealed to generate interest in the game) or within the knotted, often impossibly convoluted mysteries within the games' dungeons. Video games have always been filled with secrets, some of which were discovered only years, even decades, after the game's initial release. Many games came with secret passcodes that would unlock new characters, items or other bonuses (one particular string of button inputs featured in so many titles in the 1980s that it became known as the 'Konami code', burned into the muscle memory of every player, who would tap the inputs into a new game in order to see what, if anything, might happen). Most of these codes were, initially, designed to provide the designers with short cuts in order to test the game (extra lives, bonus powers and so on), but they were almost always left in, for players to discover.

Some secrets are ludicrously well hidden. For example, in Capcom's George A. Romero-inspired zombie game *Resident Evil 2*, a secret photograph of one of the game's characters can be found by clicking on the same oak desk no fewer than fifty times. Others are more humorous in their pay-off. In the final chapter to *Deus Ex: Invisible War*, if you flush a flag down a toilet you're warped to a dance party where all of the main (usually serious) characters can be seen dancing on stage. Other games, such as *Fez*, are entirely built around grand mysteries; their challenge is in the unpicking of the riddle.

Sometimes these mysteries go undiscovered till their creators reveal their whereabouts. Four years after *Splinter Cell: Double Agent*'s release, two of the game's developers posted a video on the internet revealing a hidden side mission, in which the characters must find and rescue four baby seals.

Whether it's to find a roaming mythical creature, or a way to bring a beloved character back from the grave, the hunt for these secrets can become obsessive. Some of the thrill is no doubt in the chance of glory for being the first to snap a Bigfoot on film, or resurrect a dead girl. But there's something else too: the comforting reassurance that the truth is out there and that, once unveiled, these mysteries are not random or without logic, but someone or something is behind them.

Video games are so good at presenting satisfying mysteries that one designer decided to use the medium to help solve one of our own world's most notorious whodunnits.

Forty-one years after the assassination of the thirty-fifth president of the United States, Kirk Ewing was about to stand trial for his murder.

'I was in Times Square sitting in the green room at *Good Morning America*,' he recalls. 'A basketball player appeared on the show before me. He'd recently punched someone in the crowd during a game and had been invited onto the programme to apologise. He made his apology and promptly announced the launch of his new rap CD.'

As the athlete left the stage and the applause died away, Ewing was ushered onto the TV programme's set. Ewing sat down and the presenter looked him in the eye. After a moment's pause, he asked: 'Why did you kill John F. Kennedy?'

Ewing is familiar with controversy. 'I've had to deal with the consequences of my actions a great deal over my life, so it was no huge surprise,' he says in a mischievous Scottish brogue. Before joining the video-game industry he worked in television, producing an episode of the current affairs programme *Dispatches* for Channel 4 and making several appearances on the long-running show *GamesMaster*.

In 2002 he worked as game director on *State of Emergency*, a game published by Rockstar Games that was denounced by Washington state politicians for replicating the 1999 World Trade Organisation riots. But *JFK: Reloaded*, a game which allowed players to assume the role of Lee Harvey Oswald, the twenty-four-year-old sniper who murdered the president on 22 November 1963, hit a different kind of national nerve. The result was controversy on a scale Ewing never anticipated.

'I was ferried by car around New York City, moving from TV station to radio station and back again,' Ewing recalls. 'For an entire week intelligent people unpicked my personality in front of an audience of millions.'

This trial by media was just the start of the onslaught.

'I had an unbelievable amount of violence directed towards me,' he says. 'There were numerous death threats in the mail. The *Daily Mail* doorstepped my parents to see what they thought about what I'd done – as if they knew what was going on. A reverend in the Midwest called me a "purveyor of electronic wickedness".

'I got that one printed on a T-shirt,' continues Ewing. 'Perhaps my favourite e-mail, the one that seems to sum up the whole ignorance around the debate, simply read: "You gay, Swedish asshole."'

Ewing's idea to create a game based on one of the most traumatic moments in recent American history was a response to what he saw as the broadening scope of most video games.

'Having worked on large video-game projects I wanted to do something smaller,' he says. 'Rather than building an enormous, expansive world I wondered about exploring a single moment in time through a game.' Ewing, who had recently set up a small studio in Scotland called Traffic Games, wanted to make a game that was based on a real-world event. 'I loved the idea that we could make games with a current affairs agenda, rather than just more stuff about orcs and goblins.'

It was also a way definitively to solve a different kind of mystery to those of Bigfoot or Aeris. This was a game that sought to put to rest the curious kind of mystery that's to be found inside a conspiracy theory.

Ewing initially considered re-creating the moon landings in video-game form.

'But JFK's assassination made the most sense because there was so much information in the public domain about what happened that day. Not only that, it was also a ballistics exercise. Video games are really good at ballistics exercises.'

Ewing was also confident that the subject matter had been discussed enough in other media to warrant a video-game approach. 'I figured: "If this subject could be discussed in film and documentary, why shouldn't it be a candidate for a game?"'

Ewing's studio was too small to take on such an ambitious project alone so he approached a friend who worked at Stainless Games, the creators of the controversial *Carmageddon* series, in which players score points by mowing down pedestrians using an overpowered car, to see whether they might partner in the development of his vision.

'My friend loved the idea,' says Ewing. 'So Stainless dusted the *Carmageddon* engine and together we did everything we could to make the most realistic interpretation of what happened that day as possible.'

The team carefully reconstructed Elm Street in Dallas, Texas, where JFK was shot, placing each lamp-post in location, and setting the wind speed and direction to reflect that day's conditions.

The team opted to ignore the conspiracy theories surrounding the assassination and to focus instead entirely on Oswald's role as the sniper.

'The more that I looked at the day's events through the lens of the game's engine the clearer it seemed to me that Oswald had fired all three shots,' Ewing says. 'In fact, part of the logic for us was to disprove the conspiracy by demonstrating how it was possible for Oswald to make all three shots in the context of the car's speed, the wind and the specification of the rifle he used. When it comes to the ballistics, I think we made a good representation of what it must have been like to look down the barrel of the gun and fire those shots at the president.'

Ewing is unequivocal when it comes to the moral dimension of the game: he sees no difference between *JFK: Reloaded* and Oliver Stone's Oscar-winning 1991 film *JFK*, which was based on the same events.

'I've mercilessly shot people in the hands or face or wherever I could get a bullet into them in countless games,' he says. 'This is no different in that sense. Beyond that, in a filmed documentary we have the position of a member of the crowd. We are there as the motorcade goes past, spectating. But in the video game, we have Oswald's perspective. For me it's valuable to look at real-life tragedy from a variety of different lenses and perspectives.'

JFK: Reloaded, as the game was titled, launched in November 2004. A demo was made freely available while the full game cost $10. In order to encourage people to invest in the full version, Ewing devised a competition around the game.

For one month players were able to submit their 'assassination attempts'. The player who most closely matched the shots taken by Oswald, as reported in the Warren Commission Report, would win a prize pot, linked to how much revenue the game had generated (up to $100,000). The final prize money amounted to just $10,712 and was won by a sixteen-year-old Parisian boy, who went by the handle 'Major_Koenig'. He posted his score the day before the competition closed.

Awarding prize money for replicating JFK's wounds is the one decision that, a decade later, Ewing regrets.

'I was naive,' he says. 'I underestimated the deepness of affection for Kennedy held by many American people. Maybe in Scotland we didn't think through the reaction. Questions about the prize money were always the toughest to answer. It was a marketing trick, but it muddied the discussion that maybe we could have had if it hadn't been there.'

That discussion, particularly in America, centred on the transgressive nature of the game, of how it trivialised a taboo subject. The right-wing news channel Fox News invited Ewing onto one of its shows and presented him with animated mock-ups of other assassinations, demanding to know why these shouldn't also be turned into video games.

'This sort of media attempts to shift the news agenda in order to create entertainment,' says Ewing. 'The whole thing is so complicit. They're using something you've created to create news stories and ratings.'

Not everyone was dismayed at the game.

'I had some touching commentary from people who wrote to me afterwards,' Ewing says. 'That day is such a powerful memory in the national consciousness that people would write to me and share what they were doing at the time, cathartically reliving the memory. In time I began to understand that, when people became upset with the game, they were generally just upset at their own memory of the events it depicts, rather than anything in particular we were doing.'

On *Good Morning America*, Ewing answered the interviewer's pointed question about why he killed the president calmly.

'I explained that I hadn't killed Kennedy because he was already dead when we made the game,' Ewing recalls. 'The guy continued: "But don't you think you're teaching children how to assassinate people?" My best response to this one was to point out that we had in fact reignited this moment in history for a nation of children who were otherwise detached from the events. That one worked sometimes . . .'

The desire to use video games as a medium for documentary, or to dispel mystery, rather than encourage it, is laudable, but *JFK: Reloaded* is difficult to class as a serious piece of work. While the game's physics were set to 'realistic' by default, the developer also included a 'chaotic' mode, whereby they're greatly exaggerated. Switch this mode on, and the game becomes a riot of crashing, bouncing cars and high-speed antics. In one fan-made YouTube movie, Jackie Kennedy can be seen being catapulted through the front windshield of the presidential limousine, before flying into the air and smashing into the sixth-floor window of a nearby building. It is as if Oliver Stone had included a series of anarchic outtakes in *JFK*'s DVD extras.

Perhaps for this reason, Ewing was awarded a solemn official condemnation from the Massachusetts House of Representatives.

'It's a beautiful document with an official seal,' he says. 'It reads: "This resolution condemns the Traffic Gaming Group for attempting to profit from the assassination of JFK and for sensationalising the tragedy of November 22nd, 1963." It's the most official document that I own. It's my degree.'

I ask Ewing whether he knows if Oliver Stone received a similar document. 'No,' he replies. 'He got the fucking Oscar instead, didn't he?'

Righteous condemnation is not the only reaction that Ewing's game has received from the establishment. A few months after the media furore died down, Ewing was invited to speak at the prestigious Sorbonne in Paris.

'I spoke in front of an unbelievably charming academic audience,' he says. 'I explained my intentions with the game and talked through what happened. When I finished I was given a standing ovation.' After the applause died down, an elderly gentleman shuffled towards the stage. 'He spoke through the translator. And do you know what he said? He said: "I think what you've done is as important as the moon landings." How's that for vindication?'

Regardless of whether you share this viewpoint, *JFK: Reloaded* resolved one mystery about the day of the assassination attempt for Ewing, at least. He believed that, from his experience playing the game, Oswald must have panicked.

'He would have been better taking the shots when the car headed towards him rather than after it turned the corner,' he says.

Many video games, especially those with vast and complicated worlds that are filled with secrets and Easter eggs, satisfy the human desire to hunt for the truth, and offer the comforting notion that there is logic and design behind these simulated worlds, the same hope that has inspired humans throughout history to search for God. Video games bear secrets left by their creators – everything from hidden codes to secret rooms – while some, like *JFK: Reloaded*, allow us to recreate the circumstances of historical mysteries in order to view them from different angles and, perhaps, happen upon a solution.

Occasionally, however, players' desire to discover game makers' secrets spills from within the virtual dimension into the real. Whether it's searching Google for clues to unreleased games, or physically turning up at a developer's door in order to find out some previously unreleased detail about a forthcoming game (as some players did during the development of *BioShock*), games encourage players to become amateur sleuths – even, in some cases, to the point of criminality.

At 6 a.m. on 7 May 2004, Axel Gembe awoke in the small German town of Schönau im Schwarzwald to find his bed surrounded by police officers bearing automatic weapons.

One officer barked: 'Get out of bed. Do not touch the keyboard.'

Gembe knew why they were there. But, bleary eyed, he asked anyway.

'You are being charged with hacking into Valve Corporation's network, stealing the video game *Half-Life 2*, leaking it onto the internet and causing damages in excess of $250 million,' came the reply. 'Get dressed.'

Seven months earlier, on 2 October 2003, Valve Corporation director Gabe Newell awoke in Seattle to find that the source code for the game his company had been working on for almost five years had leaked onto the internet. The game had been due for release a couple of weeks earlier but the development team was almost a year behind schedule. *Half-Life 2*, one of the most anticipated games of the year, was going to be late, and Newell had yet to admit to the public how late. Such a leak was not only financially threatening, but also embarrassing.

After he had spent a few moments pondering these immediate concerns, an avalanche of questions tumbled through Newell's mind. How had this happened? Had the leak come from within Valve? Which member of his team, having given years of their life to building the game, would jeopardise the project in the final hour?

If it wasn't an inside job, how did it happen? Did someone have access to Valve's internal server?

The question that rang loudest of all will be familiar to anyone who has ever had something stolen from them: who did this?

'I got into hacking by being infected myself,' Gembe tells me. 'It was a program that pretended to be a *Warcraft 3* key generator and I was stupid enough to run it. It was an sdbot, a popular general-purpose malware at the time.'

The young German soon realised what he had installed on his PC. But instead of scrubbing the malware and forgetting about it, he reverse-engineered the program to see how it worked and what it did.

By following the trail back, Gembe was able to track down its operator. Rather than confronting the man, Gembe began asking him questions about the malware.

'At the time I couldn't afford to buy games,' he explains. 'So I coded my own malware to steal CD keys in order to unlock the titles I wanted to play. It grew quickly to one of the most prominent malwares at the time, mostly because I started writing exploits for some unpatched vulnerabilities in Windows.'

In Seattle Newell's first thought was to go to the police. His second was to go to the players. At 11 p.m. on 2 October 2003, Newell posted a thread on the official *Half-Life 2* forum entitled 'I need the assistance of the community'.

Yes, the source code that has been posted is the HL-2 source code, he wrote in the post. Newell went on to outline the facts Valve had been able to piece together so far. He explained that someone had gained access to his e-mail account around three weeks earlier. Not only that, but keystroke recorders had been installed on various machines at the company. According to Newell, these had been created specifically to target Valve as they were not recognised by any virus-scanning applications.

Gembe's malware crimes, while undeniably exploitative and damaging, were crimes driven by a passion for games rather than profits. His favourite game of all was *Half-Life*. In 2002, like so many fans of the series, Gembe was eager for new details about the forthcoming sequel. That's when he had the idea: if he was able to hack into Valve's network, he might be able to find something out about the game nobody else knew yet. He would have his moment of glory but, more than that, he would have the reassurance that the game's creators had everything under control.

'I wasn't really expecting to get anywhere,' Gembe says. 'But the first entry was easy. In fact, it happened by accident.'

Gembe scanned Valve's network to check for accessible web servers where he believed information about the game might be held. 'Valve's network was reasonably secure from the outside, but their name server allowed anonymous AXFRs, which gave me quite a bit of information.'

AXFR stands for Asynchronous Full Zone Transfer, a tool used to synchronise servers. It's also a protocol used by hackers to peek at a website's data. By transferring this data, Gembe was able to discover the names of all the sub-domains of the company's web directory.

'In the port scan logs, I found an interesting server which was in Valve's network range from another corporation named Tangis that specialised in wearable computing devices,' he says. 'Valve didn't firewall this server from its internal network.'

Gembe had found an unguarded tunnel into the network on his first attempt. 'The Valve PDC had a username "build" with a blank password,' he explains. 'I was able to crack the passwords in no time. Once I had done that . . . Well, basically I had the keys to the kingdom.'

There's something about the secrets and codes that video-game developers leave in their games that allows players a kind of glimpse behind the curtain. For a moment, the game's fiction is broken and a player is able to see the cogs and workings behind the virtual world. Arguably the earliest example of an 'Easter egg' in a game was in the 1979 Atari 2600 game *Adventure*. The game was programmed by one of Atari's young employees, Warren Robinett. Like many of his colleagues, Robinett was disillusioned with his employer's policy of not crediting the game's designers and creators. He added a secret room to the game that, if discovered, revealed the text: 'Created by Warren Robinett'. It was a way to leave his own mark on the virtual world he created and, for players who first discovered the room (long after the designer left Atari), it was a link to an unseen creator.

Gembe had broken into another secret room, filled with illicit treasure. It was, as he put it, a kingdom, one that he believed would solve the *Half-Life 2* mystery.

At this point, Gembe wasn't bothered about covering his tracks. So far he had nothing to hide. But he wanted to ensure he would remain undetected as he explored further.

'All I cared about at that point was not being thrown out,' he says. 'My first job was to find a host where I could set up some sort of hideout.'

Gembe began to search for information about the game. He found various design documents and notes about the game's creation, the kind of material he hoped he might find. As the weeks passed, Gembe realised nobody at Valve had noticed he was inside the company's network. He began to push a little harder. That's when he found the ultimate prize: the source code for the game he had been waiting to play for so many years.

The temptation was too great. On 19 September 2003, Gembe downloaded the unfinished game's code and made off with Valve's crown jewels.

'Getting the source code was easy, but the game didn't run on my computer. I made some code changes to get it to run in a basic form, but it wasn't fun. Also, I only had the main development "trunk" of the game. They had so many development branches that I couldn't even begin to check them all out.'

The secret was too potent for Gembe to keep to himself. While he maintains he was not the person who uploaded the source code to the internet, he undoubtedly passed the code to the person who did.

'I didn't think it through,' he says. 'There was, of course, an element of bragging going on. But the person I shared the source with assured me he would keep it to himself. He didn't.'

Once the game was on the internet, there was no containing it.

'The cat was out of the bag,' says Gembe. 'You cannot stop the internet.'

The community's response to Newell's plea for help was mixed. While many expressed their sympathy at the theft, others felt betrayed by Valve for being led to believe the game would be ready for its scheduled launch in late 2003.

Despite a few leads, nobody was able to provide information about who might have perpetrated the crime. The FBI became involved in the investigation but also drew blanks.

Meanwhile, the team at Valve, which had been working hard to complete the game for months, was left feeling dispirited by the leak. The game was costing the company $1 million a month to build and the end was some way off. The leak had not only caused financial damage but had demotivated a weary team. One young designer asked Newell at the time, 'Is this going to destroy the company?'

At 6.18 a.m. on 15 February 2004, Valve's MD received an e-mail with a blank subject line from sender 'Da Guy'.

'Hello Gabe,' the author began, before going on to claim responsibility for infiltrating Valve's network months earlier.

Newell was unsure whether to believe the story at first. But two attached documents, both of which could only have been obtained by someone with access to private areas of Valve's server, proved the sender's claims were valid.

Five months after *Half-Life 2* was released onto the internet, long after all leads had gone cold, the thief had handed himself in.

'I was sorry for what happened,' says Gembe today. 'I wanted them to know who did this thing, and that my intention was never for things to work out the way they did.'

But that wasn't all that Gembe was after. The young man perceived a way he could create a positive outcome from his crime, both for Valve and himself. In a separate e-mail, he asked whether Newell would consider giving him a job.

'I was very naive back then,' he says. 'It was and still is my dream to work for a game-development company, so I just asked. I hoped that they could forgive what I had done, mostly because it wasn't intentional.'

To Gembe's surprise, Newell wrote back a few days later saying yes, Valve was interested. He asked whether Gembe would agree to a phone interview. The true intention of the call, however, was to obtain an on-the-record admission from Gembe that he had been responsible for the leak, an FBI trick, designed to gain a confession by appealing to a person's sense of pride.

Gembe quelled his suspicion and dialled the number he had been provided with. As far as he knew, this was an interview with two senior members of Valve's management team. In reality, the call was being taped by the FBI.

'I hoped for the best,' he says. 'I was not the brightest kid back then. At first they wanted to know how I hacked into the network. I told them in full detail. Then they asked me about my experience and skills. I still remember they were surprised that I spoke fluent English without much of an accent.'

The trio talked for forty minutes. Any sense of guilt dissipated for Gembe in the presence of his heroes. But that was nothing compared to the adrenalin rush he felt when he received an invitation to a second interview, a face-to-face meeting at Valve's headquarters in Seattle, on American soil.

Having set the trap, Valve and the FBI needed to obtain a visa for Gembe (and his father and brother, who wanted to accompany him to the US). But there were concerns about the ongoing access Gembe had to Valve's servers and the potential damage he could still cause. So the FBI contacted the German police in order to alert them to the plan.

Later that week an armed German policeman woke Gembe before dawn. He got dressed and headed downstairs. The corridors were lined by police, squeezed into his father's house.

'Can I get something to eat before we leave?' Gembe asked.

'No problem,' said one of the policemen.

Gembe reached for a kitchen knife to cut some bread. 'Every policeman in the room raised his rifle at me,' he says.

After drinking a cup of coffee and smoking a cigarette, Gembe climbed into the back of a van and was driven to the local police station. There the chief of police greeted him. He walked up to Gembe, looked him in the eye and said: 'Have you any idea how lucky you are that we got to you before you got on that plane?'

The police interrogated Gembe for three hours. 'Most of the questions they asked me were about the Sasser-Worm,' he says, referring to a particularly vicious malware that affects computers running vulnerable versions of Windows XP and Windows 2000, created by an eighteen-year-old German computer science student Sven Jaschan from Rotenburg, Lower Saxony.

'For some reason they thought there was a connection between me and Sasser, which I denied. Sasser was big news back then and its author, Sven Jaschan, was raided the same day as me in a coordinated operation, because they thought I could warn him.'

Gembe's bot exploited the same vulnerability as Jaschan's. 'Of course I denied this and told them that I never write such shoddy code,' he says.

When the police realised there was no link between Gembe and the Sasser-Worm, they began to ask him about Valve.

'I could have refused to answer and demanded an attorney, but I chose to tell them everything I knew honestly and completely, which I guess they appreciated,' he says. 'The guy questioning me liked me because he said, "You are not an asshole like most of the other guys." That department has to deal mostly with child porn. I guess I was so open with them because I didn't believe I had done much wrong, at the time.'

Gembe was remanded in custody for two weeks. He was released once the police determined he wasn't about to flee, with the proviso that he check in with them three times a week, every week, for three years, until his trial.

While waiting for his day in court, Gembe worked hard to change his life. He finished an apprenticeship and secured a job in the security sector, writing Windows applications to manage security systems and performing database and server administration work.

The trial lasted for seven hours. No one from Valve was present, though a reporter from the *Wall Street Journal* showed up. Aside from the initial theft of the game's source code, there was no evidence to suggest Gembe had been responsible for releasing the unfinished game onto the internet.

Gembe admitted to hacking into Valve's network and the judge sentenced him to two years' probation, citing his difficult childhood and the way he had worked to turn his life around as considerations when it came to deciding on the relatively lenient punishment.

By the time of the trial 8.6 million copies of *Half-Life 2* had been sold, its success unaffected by the leak of 2 October 2003.

More than a decade on from the raid, Gembe is remorseful.

'I was naive and did things that I should never have,' he says. 'There were so many better uses of my time. I regret having caused Valve Software trouble and financial loss. I regret all the illegal things I did at that time . . . And I regret not doing anything worthwhile with my life before I got busted. If I had the chance to speak to Gabe Newell today I would say this: I am so very sorry for what I did to you. You are my favourite developer, and I will always buy your games.'

While Gembe had a glimpse behind the curtain of mystery that is game development, his actions made it unlikely he will ever secure a job at a video-game company. If video games taught Gembe to hunt for secrets, this episode in his life taught him the difference between hunting for virtual secrets and commercial ones.

Most people are able to tell the difference between fiction and reality, to know that the action of shooting an image of a person in a video game is completely different from shooting a real person. But it's easier to have compassion for Gembe, a young video-game fan who, after years of hunting for secrets in video games, decided to hunt for secrets *about* his beloved video games. *Half-Life 2* became Gembe's Bigfoot, and he would do anything to prove its existence and wellbeing to the world.

The longing for truth about the world is common to all people, not just the myth-hunters, the conspiracy nuts, the amateur detectives, the bereaved or religious. Video games, as simulated worlds with well-defined rules and borders, should be devoid of mystery. Their objects and furnishings can be catalogued (each one was, after all, created by an artist), their characters placed at any time (no video-game character has ever gone missing; the computer always knows their location). Perhaps that makes the mysteries that we encounter in video games all the more alluring. We know that there is an answer out there and that somebody, be it the artist who drew Bigfoot, the writer who killed Aeris, the man who shot JFK, or the studio that made the game itself, holds the answer. And a mystery that can be solved is not only satisfying, it's also comforting.

10

HEALING

Joel Green is hysterical and there's nothing I can do about it. I try bouncing him on my knee but whenever I stop the giggles make way for fresh anguish. I try offering him a carton of apple juice. But what little fluid he manages to swallow soon comes back up, chased by curdling screams.

Many video games are power fantasies. This video game is something else. It's a puzzle without a solution. It's a game about pain, loss, fear and, ultimately, surrender. In many ways it's a *disempowerment* fantasy. Except Joel Green's story is no fantasy.

'That's how it really happened,' Ryan Green, Joel's father and the co-creator of *That Dragon, Cancer*, told me. 'We were in the hospital. Joel had acute stomach pains. It was right after that the doctors declared him terminally ill.' Within two hours Joel had become severely dehydrated and, because of the stomach bug, was unable to keep any fluids down. The pain that any parent feels when they are unable to meet the need of their child is incomparable.

'For six hours I couldn't comfort him,' said Green. 'It was a window into hell. I felt overwhelmed. I called my wife and said: "You need to come. I can't do this any more."'

When I first spoke to Green, his son Joel was four years old and fighting his third year of terminal cancer. For three-quarters of his life he had been chaotically sick. His young body had already endured a life's worth of surgery, chemotherapy and prayer. The tumours left him partially deaf and blind and, at one point, forced him to relearn how to walk. Yet Joel confounded his medical team's expectations with a resolute determination to stick with life, to endure despite it all.

Any family made to live with ongoing pain, hope and grief in this way must find a way to articulate, celebrate or simply express their experience. Some do it with photographs, home videos, written diaries or blog posts. Green, a game developer, decided to make a video game about his experience, a way to both record the journey and to try to make sense of it while he was still caught in the squall.

'It's important to me that, when I'm speaking about my journey, that I'm doing it from a "now" perspective,' says Green. 'You get a lot of wisdom in the pressure cooker. I like to think of this as a cup of water. I want to scoop it up and hand it down to someone to drink. I think I can do that more effectively in the middle of this thing than afterwards. I'm not trying to create rules for people to follow when dealing with cancer, or some potentially damaging platitude. This game is just a reflection of how I see the world, of my story.'

Back in the hospital room I lay Joel in his narrow cot, the air thick with imagined smells of antiseptic and laundry. It's the middle of the night and there are no nurses in the forsaken corridors. Joel's screams are inescapable and unfathomably distressing. This is a video game, but the real effect of a baby's suffering on the human instinct is no less diminished in unreality: everything in me longs to settle him, to meet whatever elemental need he has in this moment, to complete this most urgent of quests. Joel lies quietly on the bed for a moment. Then he smashes his head against the railings. I hunt for an 'undo' button, some floating prompt to click that will reverse the action, lift him from the crib and stop this self-harm. But the only prompt I find reads simply: 'Pray.'

Green began working on *That Dragon, Cancer* in November 2012 with his friend Josh Larson. The pair met at the 'Meaningful

Gameplay Jam', an event organised by Larson to encourage games that, in his words, have the power to 'cause someone to live differently'. In Larson, Green found an ideal teammate for this difficult project.

'Josh and I share a perspective on both games and life,' says Green. 'We are interested in telling stories that speak to the deepest things that people have to deal with. The medium is pregnant with potential to do this. Games exist at that nexus where film meets programming. Instead of passive viewing you invite people in, to actively walk with you. They can see what you saw or feel what you felt.'

We have seen how video games can provide a refuge and sanctuary for people, a place to retreat from the slings and arrows of existence, to escape and even to salve pain. But for Green and Larson, *That Dragon, Cancer* was something else. As designers, this was a place they could invite others into, in order to share their experience, to communicate the pain and uncertainty of living with a terminally ill child, and a way to celebrate that young life. For Green in particular, the project has been a way to process a painful journey, and in that process take an unusual step towards healing.

'I want people to love my son the way I love my son, and to love my son you have to meet my son,' he said. 'A video game gives the opportunity to meet my son and meet our family, and kind of walk with us in our shoes, but from a safe place.'

Back inside the game I click 'Pray' and the adult character in the scene, voiced by Green himself, utters a desperate, gutsy plea for divine intervention, something, anything, to ease the child's pain. The words are a far cry from the primary-colour pleasantries of the Sunday-school teacher; rather, it's a longing from the deepest place, a Gethsemane appeal, spat out in desperation on sore knees. As the prayer continues, Joel's cries settle into sniffles and, finally, still into mute, peaceful sleep. The relief is palpable. In that moment the player fully feels the release and freedom Green must have encountered in that room.

It's a seemingly novel moment in a video game, but is the underlying experience that different to so many virtual problems that need solving? In this early scene (just one of the many vignettes that comprise the full game) the player is presented with a problem and, by investigating their environment, must uncover the solution, in this case a *deus ex machina* in the most straightforward sense. In life, I put it to Green, even for people of faith, God does not always offer such a practical aid to tribulations. How, then, will the pair avoid making 'pray' the solution to each of the game's terminal problems?

'That is the great mystery,' says Green. 'Joel has seizures because of the chemotherapy. They are serious seizures, but he doesn't shake and drool or convulse. It's more of a head nod; his head falls forward. We pray for this to stop and, you know, the most frustrating, confusing, helpless thing for any parent is to pray and for nothing to happen. I think that's another aspect of faith: perseverance in the face of this storm that won't go away.'

Despite the centrality of faith to Green and Larson's development of the game (and the experience upon which it's based), there's no sense that *That Dragon, Cancer* is a proselytising work. 'I am trying to come from an honest place,' says Green. 'I am not trying to tell you how it should be. I am just trying to show you my perspective. Maybe it has value. I hope it does. I hope people see the world and God in a different way perhaps. But I am not out to make converts. There are universal things here that we can all understand.

'In that hospital, at two in the morning, I remember crying out. I remember my prayer changing from pleading "stop this" to becoming more of a thankful thing. Joel may have been declared terminal but he wasn't dead. That's when there was peace and he fell asleep. It's not about saying this is how it must be for everyone. It is a case of saying: this is how it happened for me.'

Video games are rarely used for autobiography, but as we have seen, their capacity to allow others to view the world from a person's perspective makes them ideally suited to the task. Not only is it possible to place a player in the shoes of another person, it's also possible in a video game to subject them to the same circumstances, pressures, powers and systems that this person experienced. How much more effective might it be, when attempting to communicate your circumstances to another, to allow them to experience those circumstances for themselves, to feel the sense of powerlessness and sorrow that Green felt directly, rather than through the more detached medium of documentary or written biography?

This is, early into the twenty-first century, unusual territory for video games. Will people truly be interested in playing a game that deals with such uncomfortable subject matter? Why would anyone want to play a game in which the person you are tasked with caring for might not make it in the end?

'That is the great risk,' Green said. 'At any point the medical team could tell us to prepare for death. I am living in the shadow of that possibility. I'm wrestling with having an ending where Joel lives or an ending where he dies. We wrote a book and our ending was: maybe he'll live to eighty. It's such a huge risk to say something like that: the reality might not match the hope. I am coming to terms with maybe being OK with that. But I am still contending for the greatest thing . . . I don't know the answer. I don't know if he dies or lives or both. Maybe we end the game before we know?'

I asked Green the hardest question: will the game's message remain the same whether Joel – the real Joel – lives or dies?

There's a painful pause.

'I hope the message doesn't change,' he replied.

We sat in silence for a while.

Then: 'Maybe it will change for a while, you know? But that's the thing with life. You go through these hard things and sometimes you deal with anger. Sometimes you deal with a feeling of injustice. Sometimes euphoria. My hope is that eventually I can step back and trust that it's going to be a good story in the end. A lot of players don't want to enter our story. Because he could die, right? And who wants to play a game about that? But I want people to trust that I am going to tell a good story regardless. Because, as difficult as it is, I am living in a *good* story.'

There are few tragic video-game stories in the classical sense. By virtue of making it to the end of the game, the player must have triumphed. (A few games, such as *Spec Ops: The Line*, play with this apparent inevitability; completing the game, a damning examination of war and its video-game depictions, makes clear that you are complicit in the downfall of the main character, and confronts you with the tremendous damage you've caused throughout the game, a pyrrhic victory at best.) Where early video games relied on the inevitability of failure to keep players adding quarters to the arcade machine's coin slot, today's players expect victory, not failure, to be the prerequisite of a video game's conclusion. But there seems to be a greater willingness in literature and cinema for creators, readers and viewers alike to approach more troubling thematic subject matter.

I wonder why Green and Larson believe people would want to play their game, to choose to experience such devastation, even second-hand.

'Hope,' says Larson. 'People search for hope in things. This is a game filled with hope. And for me personally, as a video-game player: I want to taste the full range of human experience. In books or film you get to have those experiences, to explore what it means to live. But in games we typically focus on small subsets of life. To be immersed in other situations. There's value in that.

'People reject thinking about cancer because they are ultimately afraid it's going to happen to them,' he continues. 'Nobody has a problem watching a zombie horror film because, on some level, they know that this is fantasy. But cancer is a real and present enemy to humans in this life. And it's everywhere. My journey has been characterised by coming out from under that fear. There's this scene in the movie *Rise of the Guardians* when one of the characters looks fear in the face and says: "I know who you are but I'm not afraid of you." I've feared cancer for my entire life. Then it happens. And life goes on. You learn this when you go through a great struggle. I hope people can somehow overcome their fear through this game.'

On 15 March 2014, at 1.52 in the early hours of the morning, Joel Green died.

When I heard the news I grieved. I had been there, in the hospital room when Joel was unable to find respite from the pain; I had been broken by his interminable anguish and, finally, overwhelmed with relief when he finally found rest. The news that his young life had ended, news of a death on the other side of the world, in a family with whom I had no real connection, was devastating. I thought about the family regularly as the weeks clustered into months.

Eventually, I wanted to speak to Green and Larson, to find out whether they would continue making the game or whether it had now fulfilled its function. Ever gracious, the pair agreed to speak.

'There have been emotional moments for all of us over the last months, and times where some idea is just too intense to develop. For me it was working with MRI imagery,' Larson says. 'But this season has also been very fulfilling for all of us and has brought about great clarity. Joel's passing caused us to take a step back and re-evaluate the vision as a whole. We decided to focus more on who Joel was and what it was like to be with him and to love him. This is a noticeable change from the previous direction of sharing all the ups and downs that Joel went through. Maybe another way to put it is we moved from focusing on the plot of Joel to focusing on the character of Joel.'

For Green, the game is now as much a way to preserve the memory of Joel's life as a way to invite others into the landscape of his illness.

'I want the game to capture the way Joel danced,' he says. 'The way he laughed. The way his brothers treated one another. The affection they have. I want to put those things in the game. He was the sweetest kid. I can't really articulate . . . I hope to capture some of that; some of who he was and is. In the end, I guess my greatest hope is pretty simple: that players might care about my son the way that I do.'

Most video games feature death, but only a few are *about* death. Jason Rohrer's *Passage*, released in 2007, is one of the earliest examples, a simple experimental game in which death is inevitable for the player, with no hope of respawn. In *Passage* you have, to use the video game's favoured parlance, only one life. Your character, who can move only from left to right across the screen, ages incrementally with each step. As you move through the game's landscape your character ages. You slow, at first, then the game robs you of your beauty, takes away your loved ones, slims your family. Finally, your character dies. (Rohrer told me at the time: 'I was about to turn thirty, about to witness the birth of our second child, and had just watched a neighbourhood friend wither and die from cancer. As such, I was thinking about the passage of life – and my inevitable death. I wanted to make a game that captured the feelings that I was having: existential entrapment bundled together with a profound appreciation of beauty. These are feelings that are hard to put into words.')

That Dragon, Cancer is a different kind of examination of death. It is an invitation for us to step into a family's world, in all of its turmoil, sorrow and joy. The game is not only a study of human suffering, but also a celebration of a human life, and through it anyone who is interested or affected has the opportunity to grieve and celebrate with strangers. It is, however, difficult subject matter to engage with, especially within the participatory prism of a video game, where we are no longer mere spectators to the story, but active participants within the drama. As such, while we are all invited, there's no shame in declining the invitation.

But for Christos Reid, a young game developer from the UK, and creator of *Dear Mother*, it was crucial that his intended audience showed up.

'I came out to my mother as bisexual during a temporary stay with my parents,' he explains. Reid's mother is a deeply religious person who, in his words, 'used that religion to justify her homophobia'. On hearing Reid's admission, she told her son that he was 'sick, wrong, and going to hell'.

'She told me I couldn't live in her home if I wasn't straight,' he tells me. 'And so I left.'

When Reid moved into his new home he began to try to process what he'd been through – to understand why a mother could reject her son for something over which he had no control.

'I had to deal with it, because to hold it inside me for ever seemed unwise,' he says. As a way to get the pain out of him, and perhaps to begin to process his experience, he took out his laptop and began working on a game.

'Not long later, I'd made *Dear Mother*,' he says. 'An open letter to my mum about how her beliefs had broken my heart.'

Dear Mother, which is freely available to play on the internet, is a simple game using archaic, blocky sprites to represent its characters and world, the kind you might have seen in the early 1980s. The game begins with a conversation between two characters. One, Reid's mother, begins by saying: 'My son . . . You must not sin.' The action then moves to a road outside a house. You play as a boy who must collect the angels falling from the sky, while dodging the demons, by moving left and right across the screen. A shadowy figure stands in one of the house's windows, presumably Reid's mother, watching her son as he tries to please her.

'Each devil causes your heart to break a little, and the game is structured so that, eventually, collecting enough devils to break your heart becomes unavoidable,' explains Reid. 'It's at that point that you leave, move to a new home, and you're allowed to simply collect people, instead, which heals your heart up piece by piece.'

The game has no win condition: you cannot evade a broken heart and, once you've been kicked out of home, your only choice is whether to collect healing relationships, or dodge them and remain broken-hearted. Without Reid's backstory, it's a game you'd probably ignore, but with context, it's a powerful illustration of his experience. But Reid didn't make the game for us. He made it for himself and, crucially, for his mother.

'To this day I'm not sure if my mother played it,' he says. 'I doubt she has. But I took a printout of some press coverage of the game to dinner with my father. He's never really been that interested in my games. But when he found out *Dear Mother* was about my mum, he read the article. It opened up a conversation. I'd broken a big rule in our family – to never discuss my mother's failings or abuse outside of the home.'

Reid wanted his mother to play the game in order to understand, most simply, how her actions had affected him. But he did so knowing that it was unlikely she would take an interest. As such, he also made the game for his own benefit.

'By making *Dear Mother*, I was able to finally say goodbye to someone who had been a constant source of abuse, and I was able to open the door into how I felt, without having to tell anyone directly,' he says. 'I was able to move on, having distilled my feelings into the game, and allowed people to walk a mile in my shoes by handing them a set of controls and a window into my life.'

Reid found the experience so worthwhile and helpful that he has continued to make games as a way to examine and work through things that happen to him. He is currently working on *OCDEMONS*, a game about his experience of living with OCD, and experiencing cognitive behavioural therapy in order to minimise the disorder's negative effects on his life.

'Every time I finish one of these games, I feel like I can take that issue, that part of my day-to-day that harms me, and breathe it out,' he explains. 'It's a way to take all the trials of life and turn them into a series of mechanics, both to deal with my pain in the way my artistic leanings allow me to, and to have people go "Wow, that was hard" so I can turn around and say: "Yeah, it was."'

It's not only independent creators who are willing to externalise their struggles in this way. *Papo & Yo* is a fantasy adventure game released in 2012 that was part-funded by Sony Computer Entertainment. The game was created by a team of developers led by creative director Vander Caballero, who, at the start of the game, dedicates the work to 'my mother, brothers and sister, with whom I survived the monster in my father'.

Papo & Yo begins with a rooftop chase, your schoolboy character pursuing a girl through streets filled with the mundane – wilting plants in terracotta pots, discarded footballs – but underpinned by heavy magic. Arcane symbols chalked on walls conjure staircases where there were none, while concrete walls peel back to reveal bright, ethereal nooks and cellars.

Move a discarded box two feet to the left and the building in front of you might just move in kind. It's the kind of awesome power that only a child would apply in such a modest manner – creating pathways through the city where there were none in order to win a game of chase. It's innocent, beguiling and itself acts as a metaphor for the greater message: a boy trying his best to navigate and change the landscape of an indifferent, harsh environment.

Soon enough you meet the monster that represents Caballero's father's alcoholism, a lumbering ugly giant that is entirely docile at rest, but who becomes enraged when he licks one of the frogs that pepper the game world.

The story is lightly told, the cut-scenes sparse and dialogue fleeting. Every so often, the director breaks to a flashback, a scene that makes clear the tragic consequence of his father's addiction in real life. But the gentle tone elsewhere ensures that the moments when the elephant in the room is addressed are all the more affecting.

'He cannot control himself,' says the boy after the monster's first uncontrollable rage – one part statement of fact, one part defence.

'There is a cure,' says his companion, a young girl.

'Cure? How?' he asks her.

'Only you can cure the monster.'

'But I don't know anything,' he pleads.

It's unclear whether the scene is supposed to be a conversation between the boy and his conscience – that hopeful, yearning side to any child who lives with a parent who cannot control their demons. But this is inescapably a game about a child trying to save the unsaveable, assuming a confused role and an impossible task that no boy should ever have to take on, and yet which so many do.

When asked by a journalist why he chose to turn his experiences into a game, Caballero said: 'It was my love for games, I think. When I was a kid and going through difficult times, games actually saved me. It was the only space where I could be in control and experience safety, and predictability in a way. Everything outside was crazy.'

As with *That Dragon, Cancer*, there's a sense of discomfort when playing *Papo & Yo*. You have been invited into a cathartic exercise (Caballero's therapist even makes a cameo in the game). When film directors work out their grief, anger or resentment on the screen, you spectate. With *Papo & Yo*, you participate in this therapeutic endeavour, and while that can lead to a sense of disquiet, it also elicits empathy as you enter into the healing process.

For Green, Reid and Caballero, game-making has been a way to externalise their experiences, a way, perhaps, to recreate the situation in virtual form so that it can be examined, replayed, maybe even controlled. It seems clear that the medium's power is not only in allowing us to experience the world from another's perspective, but also in providing us with a way to replay our own experiences in order to better understand them, much like a patient in a psycho-therapist's chair, revisiting past moments in a safe place.

If video games are able to help us to understand complex systems and positions in life that are different to our own, it's logical that some would try to use them as a way to make sense of their grief and trauma and to invite others into their experience. The creators of *Papo & Yo*, *Dear Mother* and *That Dragon, Cancer* have decided to make their games public. In this way and to different degrees of vulnerability and, arguably, success, they share their burden, life and story with others.

But therapeutic game-making is not only a perfomative art. In some cases, it's both deeply personal and entirely private.

In the autumn of 2006 the game designer Brenda Romero suffered what she describes as a severe assault. In the weeks following the attack she lay numb in bed.

'I chain-watched *Grey's Anatomy* because I couldn't think,' she said during a talk entitled 'The prototyping of tragedy' delivered at the 2011 Game Developers Conference, the only time that she has spoken publicly, albeit in brief, about the attack. Her mind, she recalled at the time, was immobile in the shadow of one unanswerable question: 'Why the *fuck* would someone like that do something like this to someone like me?'

After a while lying with the pain and confusion, she began to tackle the question in the only way that she knew how: through game design.

'I didn't want to live with this thing in me, so I started to explore pain and evil as a system,' she tells me. 'I started designing a video-game level in my head. I thought maybe this would help me to understand.'

That Romero would try to make sense of her trauma within the framework of a game is, she says today, entirely understandable.

'When you join the games industry at the age of fifteen it's the way that you make sense of the world. If I were a musician I might write a song. If I was a writer I might write an article. But I am a game designer: I *have* to process systemically.'

As the weeks passed, more games began to come to Romero, games that sought to explain the systems that drove the world's tragedies and injustices both contemporary and historical: the slave trade, Oliver Cromwell's invasion of Ireland in the seventeenth century and that most imponderable of all humanity's great blights: the Holocaust. Her suffering seeded in her a new approach to game design, a hopeful way to make sense of the senseless.

Then, in 2009, she played *The Path*, a psychological horror game inspired in part by the Little Red Riding Hood fairy tale, and another of the art games released by *Endless Forest* creators Tale of Tales.

'There's a part in the woods when a guy walks up to you,' she recalls. 'The only thing I could think was: "Fuck, I am going to get raped."'

It was a feeling that Romero had not experienced in a video game before.

'It was a painful and repellent trigger,' she says now, 'but for reasons I don't recall, I didn't shut down and shut out. For some reason, I stayed there and felt through it . . . and I began to feel some kind of relief, some kind of peace.'

Romero has been working on video games for most of her life. She joined Sir Tech, a developer based in Ogdensburg, a small dairy town on the outskirts of New York, in 1981 at the age of fifteen. Romero – née Garno – spent the next twenty years working at the company, first manning the tips phone line to give gamers who were stuck in one of the company's games guidance, and later as a game designer and programmer. In 1987 she met John Romero, the co-creator of the seminal first-person shooter *Doom* and the man who, twenty-five years later, she would marry.

Just one year before the attack she spoke about at the 2011 Game Developers Conference, Romero was working on a crass *Playboy* game. A few years later, *Train*, Romero's board game about the systemic and systematic extermination of the Jews in Nazi death camps, was celebrated by a rabbi as a work of Torah, a part of the canon of Jewish teaching and culture. She has become game designer in residence at the University of California, Santa Cruz's Center for Games and Playable Media. But despite all of this success, today, after she returns home from her day job at the social game company Loot Drop, which she co-founded with her husband in 2010, she works on *Black Box*.

'It's the game with which I wanted to first understand evil systems and the bad things that happen to us,' she says, a 'Ground Zero' game, from which all of the others have sprung.

Black Box is the last of a suite of six deeply personal games, which Romero groups together under the title 'The mechanic is the message'. Each of the games is a physical creation, something between a board game and an art installation, and in each case the player is provided with a framing narrative, but free to draw their own conclusions.

To date, three have been made public: *The New World*, a game about slavery created in 2008; *Síochán leat* (Gaelic for 'Peace be with you'), Romero's 2009 release about Oliver Cromwell's invasion of Ireland; and, most famously, *Train*, the board game about the Holocaust.

In *Train* the player is presented with a set of miniature train tracks and sixty small yellow pegs that represent people. The player is asked to efficiently load those people onto the trains. You can follow the rules, if you wish, but maybe you don't have to. At the point at which the player successfully completes the game, they overturn a card that reveals the train's destination: Auschwitz. The player's high of winning is immediately punctured by the stark realisation that they have been complicit in loading Jews onto box cars (one yellow peg represents 100,000 Jews) en route to the infamous concentration camp where 1.1 million were killed in gas showers or burned in ovens during the Second World War.

Romero researched the Holocaust extensively. Each day during the nine months that it took to design *Train*, she stared at a picture of two boys wearing the Star of David that the Nazis required that Jews wear for identification. She imagined that she was the boys' mother. She'd mentally straighten their clothes. She'd project.

Most feel shame when they play the game. Some hide, some cry, some attempt to subvert the rules. Holocaust survivors have played *Train*. For Romero, post-2006, tragic subject matter is not taboo.

'You can't have human tragedy at any scale without a system,' she says. 'And if you give me a system, I can make you a game.'

Some have not shared her point of view. 'I had people telling me I should fucking leave the games industry,' she tells me, 'or that I should be punched in the face, or that they hope I realise how much pain I've brought to people.' Many others, including the rabbi, responded more positively. The game was featured in museums, lauded by educators and given a Vanguard award at the IndieCade festival for 'pushing the boundaries of game design and showing us what games can do'.

Having explored human tragedy at the macro scale, now, at last, Romero is circling *Black Box*, the most 'difficult' game in the series and the most localised and personal. It's a game designed to be played one time, by one player. Romero intends to be that player. Once the game has been played, it cannot be played again, although others will be able to view the endgame state.

'*Black Box* is about the worst experience of my life,' she says. 'I am not going to talk about what the game is about; that's why it's in a black box. When I finish the game I may invite several of my friends and explain what it's about.'

For Romero, these are the games that she has to birth into the world, to get them out of her. *Black Box* has cost more than a thousand dollars to make and it's something that cannot be sold. It's played inside a two-by-two-foot black plexiglas cube. It sits on a platform and is subtly lit from underneath. 'When you look inside you can see forty figures,' she explains.

'In the centre of these figures is a smaller one. On top of the black box is an adding machine. The adding machine says 1, 4, 5, 10, 10, 10 then it says 40 and repeats that number endlessly on the paper as it spills down to the floor.'

Romero's kitchen is currently littered with inch-tall figures, tokens that will be used in the game, the debris of her memory, slowly being ordered and arranged into game form. It seems to be a way to, if not make sense of evil, then at least to place it within a system where it can be controlled and mastered.

This is, for many, the great appeal of all games: to experience a reality that runs on unflinching logic and justice, where the rules are never broken, where randomness can be contained and tamed. As

Caballero put it, in the midst of chaos, games are sometimes the only available space where one can be in control and experience safety and predictability.

But it's more than that, too; these games elicit not only understanding, but also personal healing. We have seen how video games offer a compelling and comforting refuge from life's trials. But the opportunity for escapism isn't their only offering. For their creators they can also offer a way to process grief, trauma and turmoil, a safe prism in which to experience or, at least, move towards healing.

And for those of us who choose to enter into the game maker's story, there's an opportunity to understand and perhaps move towards healing some of our own wounds too.

11

SURVIVAL

INSERT COIN TO CONTINU

Morgan van Humbeck completed his shift in front of the television and passed out. Ten minutes later, his cell phone woke him.

'Morgan, this is Teller,' said a voice on the other end of the line.

'Fuck off,' van Humbeck replied in disbelief.

He hung up the phone and went back to sleep.

The drive from Tucson, Arizona, to Las Vegas, Nevada, takes approximately eight hours when travelling in a vehicle whose top speed is forty-five miles per hour. In *Desert Bus*, an unreleased video game from 1995 conceived by the American illusionists and entertainers Penn Jillette and Teller, players must complete that journey in real time. Finishing a single leg of the trip requires considerable stamina and concentration in the face of arch-boredom: the vehicle constantly lists to the right, so players cannot take their hands off the virtual wheel; swerving from the road will cause the bus's engine to stall, forcing the player to be towed back to the beginning.

The game cannot be paused. The bus carries no virtual passengers to add human interest, and there is no traffic to negotiate. The only scenery is the odd sand-pocked rock or road sign. Players earn a single point for each eight-hour trip completed between the two cities, making a *Desert Bus* high score perhaps the most costly in the medium. Van Humbeck, again unconscious on the couch, had just contributed to what was then a *Desert Bus* world record: five points.

Whenever Penn and Teller were booked to appear on the David Letterman show, a close friend, Eddie Gorodetsky, the Emmy Award-winning television writer whose credits include *The Fresh Prince of Bel-Air, Two and a Half Men* and *Saturday Night Live*, would visit their office and pretend to be Letterman to help them prepare. During one of these rehearsals, the trio came up with the concept of a video game that could work as a satire against the anti-video-game lobby.

'Every few years, video games are blamed in the media for all of the ills in society,' Teller tells me. 'In the early 1990s, I wrote an article for the *New York Times* citing all the studies that show video games have no effect on a child's morals. But we wanted to create some entertainment that helped make the point.'

The conversation with Gorodetsky seeded the idea of a video game that casts the player as a bus driver in a rote simulation. Where most game designers choose the extremities of life for their metaphor, Penn and Teller were interested in the most mundane and irritating job they could imagine.

'The route between Las Vegas and Phoenix is long,' says Teller. 'It's a boring job that just goes on and on repetitiously, and your task is simply to remain conscious. That was one of the big keys – we would make no cheats about time, so people like the Attorney General could get a good idea of how valuable and worthwhile a game that just reflects reality would be.' (The US Attorney General at the time, Janet Reno, was a vociferous critic of on-screen violence.)

The New Jersey-based video-game developer Imagineering created *Desert Bus* as one component of a larger game collection, called *Penn & Teller's Smoke and Mirrors*, for the Sega CD, a short-lived add-on for the Sega Genesis console. Penn, Teller and the game's publisher, Absolute Entertainment, planned a lavish prize for any player who scored a hundred points, a feat that would require eight hundred continuous hours of play: a real-life trip from Tucson to Las Vegas on a desert bus carrying showgirls and a live band.

'But by the time the game was finished, the format was dead,' says Teller. 'We were unable to find anybody interested in acquiring the game.'

Imagineering went out of business, and *Penn & Teller's Smoke and Mirrors* was never released. The only record of the game's existence was a handful of review copies that had been sent out to journalists in the weeks before the publisher went bust, in 1995.

The game remained a rumour until September 2005, when Frank Cifaldi, a freelance American journalist and self-professed video-game historian, received a package in the mail. Cifaldi is the founder of Lost Levels, a website dedicated to the preservation of rare and obscure video games.

'The site attracted the attention of some people who happened to have copies of unpublished games they didn't know what to do with,' he explained. 'One guy who used to review games for a magazine in the 1990s still had his review copy of *Smoke and Mirrors*.' Cifaldi posted a review and a copy of the game to a number of internet forums. *Desert Bus* had been rediscovered.

Humanity's oldest quest is survival. We eat, drink, fight and re-produce in service to this quest, passing on our DNA to each successive generation, ensuring that we survive, not only in life, but also in death. It's logical, then, that the quests found in our video games reflect this daily undertaking, from which no living thing can escape. From the earliest titles in the arcades, video games have tasked players with staving off the inevitable 'game over' screen, that black, mournful purgatory into which we are deposited when our virtual opponents (be they space invaders, enemy soldiers or a rival football team) get the better of us.

Almost all video games have this survival element coded within their rules and 'losing' a game is usually closely linked to some idea of death. Video-game designers routinely employ the metaphor of life and death in their game's terminology: characters have 'lives' (when they are depleted, you are 'over'; do well in the game and you often earn extra lives, second chances that prolong your journey and provide a buffer from death), or 'health', usually represented by hearts.

In many games you replenish this health with food (*Gauntlet*), medicine (*Halo: Combat Evolved*) or bandages (*Dead Rising*). The language of survival is used across the medium with such regularity that we no longer notice its origins.

Some games turn the character into a ghost when they 'die' (*Spelunky*) while others, such as *Demon's Souls*, make you return to the site of your most recent 'death' in order to collect the items you dropped there. Other video-game characters, such as *Worms*, mark the spot of their passing with a gravestone. In *Cannon Fodder*, for each of your soldiers that perish during a mission a new grave is added to a virtual hillside, a mark of their death (as well as an indication of the cumulative human cost of your various sorties). This language, both written and visual, infuses video games with primal urgency that we instinctively respond to; it's a kind of shorthand by which a designer can indicate to a player that the stakes are tremendously high. They suggest that the loss is ultimate, even if, in the majority of cases, it is merely a temporary setback.

Eugene Jarvis, one of the most influential game designers of the 1980s, once said: 'All the best video games are about survival – it's our strongest instinct, stronger than food, sex, lust for money.' (Jarvis's best-known game, *Defender*, makes the player responsible not only for his or her own survival, but also that of human characters, who must be carefully rescued.) Whether or not the central quest of survival makes for the best games is debatable, but survival is indisputably the dominant underlying quest of video games, from *Space War* in the 1960s, all the way up to the latest military-themed blockbusters.

Video-game survival comes in many different guises. In *Geometry Wars* you play as a bright speck, trying to outmanoeuvre a firework display of angry particles. *DayZ* is a post-apocalyptic scavenger hunt, in which players forage in the countryside, trading tins of beans, packets of biscuits and scarce ammunition with people they meet, never quite sure whether the player they're trading with will shoot them the moment their back is turned. *The Binding of Isaac* is a game about surviving the shifting mazes of an underground basement. Here enjoyment comes from being able to react to unexpected threats (which change with every play-through). Part of the appeal of this kind of survival challenge is the chance to learn and improve in a safe, consequence-free space. Like the lion cub, play-fighting with its parent, learning how to handle itself, move, pounce and bite, we are somehow learning how to improve our chances of survival within a virtual dimension, perhaps so that we might better master survival in our own.

Not all kinds of survival in video games are so primal. *Desert Bus* explores a different kind of survival still: that of endurance in the face of terminal boredom. Its challenge is that of persisting with a mundane task, the kind of situation we might face at our place of work. This kind of survival has to do with persistence, not for one's life, but for one's livelihood. And, in *Desert Bus*, some players were inspired to test just how long they could persist.

Van Humbeck is a former member of LoadingReadyRun, an internet sketch-comedy group founded by Graham Stark and Paul Saunders in 2003.

'I heard about *Desert Bus* in early 2006, on a website called waxy. org,' Saunders tells me. 'The blog post linked to an extensive description of the main game, as well as the various mini-games included on the disc – and, most importantly, it had a torrent of the entire game available for download.'

Saunders wanted to film the group as it attempted to complete *Desert Bus* for a sketch. But another of the team members, James Turner, had another idea. He suggested that, in the group's quest to survive the monotony of the game, they might have a chance to join in a survival project on this side of the screen. He suggested using the game as a way to benefit Child's Play, a charity that donates video games and consoles to children's wards in hospitals around the world.

'His idea was a live competition event where we would take pledges depending on how far we made it in various video games,' says Saunders. 'We decided to combine both ideas and play *Desert Bus* for charity.'

Desert Bus for Hope, as the event was dubbed, was scheduled to begin late November 2007, and Saunders built a simple website to promote its existence.

'I initially called the website "The First Annual Desert Bus for Hope", but only because I thought it sounded funny,' he says. 'We hadn't thought about repeating the event at this point.'

For every donation they received, the group pledged to drive a portion of the game's route between Tucson and Las Vegas. They would film their progress and live-stream it on the internet.

'The event itself was very cobbled together in the first year,' explains Stark. 'The camera's wide-angle lens was held on with rubber bands.' On the weekend of the event, Saunders and Stark set up the camera and a Sega CD system, and embarked on the first leg of the virtual journey.

'They didn't contact us,' says Teller. 'Someone sent me a news story about the event over e-mail. So I got in contact.'

Saunders e-mailed Teller back, thanking him for his interest. He asked whether Teller might consider giving the team an encouraging phone call to inspire what had become a 'hub of sleep deprivation'.

After Morgan van Humbeck hung up on him, Teller found another number to reach the team, and asked what they'd like for lunch.

'They sent me the menu for a local Chinese restaurant,' Teller recalls. 'I made the calls and had it all delivered.' Teller called back every day to buy the group lunch; he and Penn each donated five hundred dollars.

'That first year, we had no plans for food or scheduling,' says Stark. 'If it hadn't been for friends and family coming by with food, and to just hang out and keep us awake, I don't think it would have succeeded.' The team managed to score five points in a hundred and eight hours of continuous play before a driver, in the fug of drowsiness, crashed the bus.

'When we discussed our fund-raising goal, we decided to aim for one thousand dollars,' says Stark. 'But I lobbied to increase our goal to five thousand dollars, to give our viewers something crazy to reach for. We raised twenty-two thousand and eighty-five dollars that year.'

Desert Bus for Hope is now in its tenth year, and has raised more than a million dollars.

'I liken it to AIDS walks,' says Teller. 'When they first started, I think everyone was quite puzzled by them. Then people began to understand that performing a mundane task and having someone sponsor you is an interesting way to raise money.'

Nevertheless, both Saunders and Stark struggle to understand the game's efficacy.

'I have friends involved in worthwhile charities that struggle for every twenty-dollar donation,' said Saunders. 'But *Desert Bus for Hope* seems to operate in this strange alternate universe where you can challenge strangers on the internet to donate five thousand dollars in the next five minutes, and the money seems to just suddenly appear.' Teller said that at a recent magic show, 'a guy came up to me and handed me a hundred-dollar bill and asked, "Would you get this to the guys that do *Desert Bus*?"'

'The game isn't the challenge for us; it's the excuse to keep us all trapped in a room for a week,' Stark explains. 'It's the horrible glue that binds the whole event together. I've achieved a Zen-like state while playing it, where it doesn't bother me as long as I don't think about it. If I do think about it, it's goddam awful.'

Saunders agrees, mournfully: 'It is, without a doubt, the very worst video game I have ever played.'

Desert Bus isn't the only desert-based video game whose appeal remains somewhat unclear to its players. *Desert Golfing*, launched for iPhones in 2014, is another game set in an arid locale, with an indefinite end point, which has also inspired the devotion of a huge following of players.

Like *Minecraft*, with its familiar rhythms of day and night, and familiar urges to stave off predators, and scavenge, *Desert Golfing* is a straightforward video game. But the emotional journey for its player is far more complicated. And it's in this psychological journey that we can perceive something of the enduring appeal of survival games.

Here's how it goes. You begin with the eager anticipation that immediately precedes the playing of all video games: the hope that you are about to be challenged, surprised and thrilled by the work. For the first eighteen holes, these hopes are quietly met, accompanied by (for players of a certain age, at least) a sense of nostalgia at *Desert Golfing*'s Atari-chic aesthetic and impossibly simple control scheme (press your finger to the phone or tablet's glass; pull back to smearily set the ball's power and angle; release to putt).

With confidence comes the urge to improve. It's now not enough to merely land the ball in the hole: you have to do so quickly and efficiently in as few shots as possible. You begin to read the power meter properly, to better judge the angles, to pull off the odd joyous hole-in-one. With mastery comes the desire to reset the game and start over with your newly acquired knowledge. But here *Desert Golfing* defies convention: there is no restart button, no option to exit and begin again. In fact, there is no menu at all.

Now comes the bitter realisation that, in contrast to other video games, which so generously allow us to remake our history till we perfect our story, in this wilderness you must live with your mistakes. The realisation is simple but profound: your past scorecard cannot be undone; you only have power to change the future.

Resignation comes next. Then, if you're sensible, reconciliation. You learn to forgive your past self, that idiot who took all those hubristic, arcing shots, who so gleefully went for the thunderous hole-in-one when he should have putted his way to lesser, more bankable glories. Now, as you reach hole 150-odd, you find resolve. You're lining up shots with care, but the real game takes place, as Bobby Jones famously put it, on the five-and-a-half-inch course between your ears.

You obsessively divide your total number of shots by the number of holes you've completed. Can you maintain an average of three per hole or less? This state persists every time you slide out your phone to get a few tees in while standing at the supermarket checkout till, or queuing at the post office behind a phalanx of texters.

At some point you become weary of the grind. Yet there is the dim awareness that, just maybe, there is nobility in the fact you've made it to hole 1,687. You take to social media to share your progress. The preening only draws the other *Desert Golfers* out. In turn they post *their* screenshots, proving how much farther they've travelled down the rabbit hole. The moment of irritation is short-lived; it soon thickens into grim resolve. You head back into the wilderness and *you persist*. This simple, throwaway game is complicated. *Desert Golfing* isn't so much a good walk spoiled as the gaming of survival.

Inspiration for *Desert Golfing* came to Justin Smith, an independent game designer from Vancouver, Canada, when playing *Journey*, Sony's PlayStation 3 game about death and religion in the desert.

'I wanted to add golf to *Journey* in the same way someone would draw a moustache on the *Mona Lisa*,' explains Smith. 'The terrain in that game was perfect for golf, and I thought golf would add a quantifiable purpose.' Smith 'let the idea sit for a while' and then began to realise his vision in the bold 2D graphics of 1980s computer games. 'The colour palette for *Desert Golf* is actually borrowed from *Journey*, but I figured it would be best not to call it *Journey Golfing*.'

At first Smith wanted to limit the game to a thousand holes. Rather than manually design these he wrote an algorithm to randomise their layout 'as a survival technique'. Smith already had the name for the game, taking inspiration from *Desert Bus*. He then decided to draw further inspiration from Penn and Teller's game by making it interminably long and repetitive.

Smith, who taught himself to programme by typing code listings from the back of magazines into the Sinclair 1000 that his grandmother bought him one Christmas, made the decision to prevent restarting the game early on.

'Adding a way to start over would sap some of the fun out,' he says. 'If you're doing poorly, the temptation to hit the reset button would always be lurking over you. But with no way to restart, the player feels a sense of freedom and reconciliation with life's past mistakes.'

That sense of freedom and reconciliation was reflected in Smith's own process of designing the game – which took just eight days from start to finish. The greatest challenge was, he says, to resist the temptation to add in 'indulgent' features such as curved slopes, power-ups and wind.

'Not all the holes are enjoyable,' he says. 'There are some very repetitive ones. And I did nothing to ensure that an impossible hole wouldn't be generated. In fact, there's a hole in the late 2000s that I was certain was impossible, a sudden ending in the middle of the desert. Of course: never underestimate players. They got past it.'

Since the game's launch players have been 'getting past it' in droves. The game has no end (the algorithm created infinite courses). But as Smith didn't expect anyone to make it past the hole in the late 2000s, 'what comes after is just patterns in white noise'. This hasn't stopped one player from making it past the five thousandth hole, surviving against the odds.

'Nobody should go that far,' says Smith. 'I'm saying it now so I don't feel responsible for more wasted time: there is officially nothing of interest past the three thousandth hole.'

Or is there? Because much of what makes *Desert Golfing* interesting exists independently of Smith's intentions. The player's journey through resignation to resolve is one that takes place in the mind; the desert's landscape is secondary. Sure, it is here, among the dunes, that the game pricks some key interests in the player, the mystery of what lies ahead, the joy of discovering a new place, a new subtlety, a new rhythm in the play experience.

But the desert is a mere backdrop for the mind games of perseverance in the face of hostility or futility, that very same urge that drives any human to endure.

Video games offer us a place in which to practise the art of survival, be it in familiar circumstances (the domestic environment of *The Sims*) or alien ones (*Mass Effect*, *Halo*, *Call of Duty*). Human beings are adaptable and ingenious, and video games allow us to explore the bounds of this adaptability and ingenuity; a way for us to feel clever about our aptitude or talent for survival, not to mention a way to compare our survival scores with our peers (regardless of whether that score is recorded in points, seconds lasted or holes completed).

Maybe the incontrovertible evidence of the video-game high-score table acts as a way to prove to others our aptitude for survival, to advertise by quantitative measure our power and suitability as a mate. High scores allow us to create a pecking order; they describe who is the fastest, the strongest, the quickest, the most adaptable, the most likely to survive for the longest.

Video games, of course, present a different sort of opportunity to survive for the people who create them. In Ernest Becker's Pulitzer Prize-winning 1973 book *The Denial of Death*, the late psychologist argued that all human civilisation is an elaborate, symbolic defence mechanism against our mortality. If we have children as a way to preserve our DNA and values, then we create art and entertainment (and even engage in acts of heroism) as a way to preserve our names, thoughts, ideas and perspectives.

'The real world is simply too terrible to admit,' wrote Becker. 'It tells man that he is a small trembling animal who will someday decay and die. Culture changes all of this, makes man seem important, vital to the universe. Immortal in some ways.'

This much is true of all game makers: in their creations they are able to make tiny worlds that reflect their interests, values and skills. But for one group of indigenous American people who, in 2014, began to design their own video game, the goal to survive through art was more deliberate and pointed than for most.

For more than three thousand years, the Iñupiat people of Alaska have passed on stories to their children. Like all enduring fiction, the stories deliver truths that transcend cultural shifts. They act as seeds of moral instruction and help to define and preserve the community's identity. The story of Kunuuksaayuka, for example, is a simple tale of how our actions affect others: a boy named Kunuuksaayuka goes on a journey to identify the source of a savage blizzard. In the calm eye of the storm, he finds a man heaving shovelfuls of snow into the air, oblivious that they gather and grow into the squalls battering Kunuuksaayuka's home downstream.

The Iñupiat's oral tradition, however, is at risk. Over the past few decades, advances in technology and communication have opened up the community to a flood of other stories delivered in new ways.

'As is common for indigenous peoples who are also part of a modern nation, it's been increasingly difficult to maintain our traditions and cultural heritage,' Amy Fredeen, the CFO of both E-Line Media, a publisher of educational video games, and of the Cook Inlet Tribal Council (CITC), a non-profit group that serves the Iñupiat and other Alaska natives, told me. 'Our people have passed down knowledge and wisdom through stories for thousands of years – almost all of this orally – and storytellers are incredibly respected members of society. But as our society modernises it's become harder to keep these traditions alive.'

For the CITC, the challenge was to find a way to preserve

the community's stories in a way that could withstand modernity. As the team pondered the problem over lunch a few years ago, the council's CEO, Gloria O'Neill, suggested a video game. O'Neill had been looking at examples of indigenous communities expressing their heritage through modern forms – such as the film *Whale Rider*, which explores gender roles in Maori culture – and was considering whether the medium could help to preserve the Iñupiat's cultural heritage. 'We all agreed that, if done well, a video game had the best chance of connecting native youth with their cultural heritage,' Fredeen says. Moreover, the council believed that a video game offered a chance to share the community's stories and culture with new audiences around the world. 'Our stories feature strong characters, fascinating settings, and are filled with wisdom and learning that address universal human themes. We believe they can travel.'

In conjunction with E-Line, the CITC founded Upper One Games, the first indigenous-owned video-game company in the United States.

'We looked at a range of options for reaching the community's business and creative goals,' Sean Vesce, a creative director at the company, tells me. 'We quickly settled on the idea of a game inspired by and based on the rich storytelling traditions and culture of the Iñupiat people. The climate in which they live is some of the most remote and extreme on the planet. We were immediately drawn to their world view, traditions and values, and how that might translate into a video game.'

With any creative project in which a group of privileged Westerners look to recount the tales and customs of an indigenous group, there is a risk of caricature, even amiable racism.

'We've repeatedly seen our culture and stories appropriated and used without our permission or involvement,' Fredeen said.

'People were sceptical that the project would turn out like these other examples, all appropriation and Westernization.' To reassure them, the development team assembled a group of Iñupiat elders, storytellers and artists to become partners in the game's development and lend their ideas and voices to the venture.

'As it became clear to the community that this project was only going to move forward with their active participation, that hesitancy quickly evaporated,' Fredeen says. 'We've had everybody from eighty-five-year-old elders who live most of the year in remote villages to kids in Barrow High School involved in the project.'

The result is *Never Alone* (*Kisima In itchu a* in the Iñupiat language). In the game, players switch between the role of a girl named Nuna and her pet Arctic fox. Each character has a different set of skills, and the pair must work together to overcome obstacles on a journey that mirrors the one taken by Kunuuksaayuka, the blizzard investigator. This theme of interdependence is central to Iñupiat stories, no doubt born of the need to help one another in order to survive the harsh Alaskan conditions. It's a message *Never Alone* seeks to impart through both its spoken narration (which has been recorded in Iñupiat) and the unspoken story communicated by its rules and mechanics.

For Vesce and the rest of the game's development team, partnering with amateur game makers was unusually challenging.

'To make *Never Alone*, we had to break from some traditional and fundamental ways of making games and bring the community into the creative process – a community that knew very little about the medium but that had strong thoughts on what they wanted to see in a game based on their culture,' Vesce says. He calls this kind of collaboration 'inclusive development', in which each group is a student of the other's world. 'While it's extremely rewarding, it also requires a huge commitment from all sides to build a foundation of mutual trust and respect.'

Despite the importance of keeping the Iñupiats' vision for the project, there was no formal approval process during development.

'It was more subtle, involving conversations with many different people, soliciting and gauging reactions to ideas, and finding creative solutions to meet both the community's goals and our goals as game developers,' Vesce says. 'When we encountered things that sounded great to us as game developers but didn't resonate with our community partners, they would often present alternatives that ended up being much more interesting and often more challenging to incorporate.'

Never Alone's purpose is to preserve fading stories. It's a way not only for a game maker to survive, as per Becker's definition, through their work of art, but also for an entire tradition and world view to survive through the representation. It's a worthy ambition, but in order to convince the Iñupiat young people of the stories' enduring power and worth, it must also succeed as a video game. In a sense, it was perhaps the riskiest way of approaching the Iñupiat's problem: this kind of storytelling requires an entirely new vocabulary. Reconciling narrative demands with the need to be engaging and functional remains one of the greatest challenges in game development; it's a struggle for even the largest and best-funded teams.

As we have seen, video games are well suited, however, to render in exquisite detail historical places and periods, and even the societies within them – the environments and systems that facilitate story creation in the first place. Players are often cast as a game's protagonist, with an active role in its story, where they cannot help but see things, at least superficially, from a new perspective. *Never Alone*, if nothing else, offers a way, however incomplete, to experience life as an Iñupiat girl, eliciting the kind of empathy that we have seen games can generate in unique and powerful ways.

There's another memorable line in *The Denial of Death*, a book built from columns of memorable lines.

'People create the reality they need in order to discover themselves,' Becker writes in a truth that's dispensed with enviable brevity. This thought is especially pertinent to the video-game maker, who is in the business of reality creation. There is something here that links *Desert Bus* to *Desert Golfing* to *Never Alone* (as well as, of course, all of those games built for therapeutic reasons, in or through which their creators hope to find understanding and healing), all of which are games based in hostile environments, where survival is a challenge, where reality bears down on the human. They are adverse realities, to which humans are drawn. In games we can find a resilience to survive against all odds. In *Desert Bus* it's expressed as stoicism in the face of the stultifying rhythms of monotony found in a repetitious task. In *Desert Golfing* it's in mastering the mind games of a seemingly endless mission. And in *Never Alone*, it's about preserving a memory.

Survival is the foundation stone that underpins all video games. They offer a quick and easy reassurance of our capacity to endure, to have second chances, to survive. Even if we fail, if Mario loses his final life on a hill in the Mushroom Kingdom, or if Lara Croft misjudges a leap and falls to her death at the bottom of some forgotten tomb, there's always another go. Even the most punitive games, such as *Steel Battalion*, a Japanese game that famously erases your character's saved progress when he 'dies', allow you to restart the game from the beginning. Video games soften reality's bite by giving us the reassurance that there's always another go: the extra life, the time extend, the 'continue'.

There is a somewhat grim irony to this idea in the context of the Taiwanese café deaths. If we play video games in order to gain a sense of immortality, or at the very least to practise the art of survival, how tragic when a video game plays a role in the death of its player. In these cases the illusion proves not only treacherous, but untrue.

Nevertheless, it's an illusion that, for a moment at least, pulls our thoughts away from the ultimate truth: life on this earth is fatal.

12

UTOPIA

INSERT COIN TO CONTINUE

The video game denies our mortality. Every game is a virtual reality that reflects our own world in some way, and yet every game also eradicates the one certainty of existence: its finality. Within a video-game representation you will often find echoes of life's fragility. But you will never experience true extinction. There is always another life to be lived.

If, through video games, we have found a way to confound death itself, surely the video game has the capacity to correct other injustices of our world? This is, after all, the inexhaustible wonder of the medium: the capacity to make tangible any type of reality that can be imagined, whether that is a world on fire, one beset with aliens, or something more peaceful and just.

Video games are normally based on fairer and more just systems than those in the real world (or, at very least, systems that tend to favour the player). That's what makes them so palatable, such wonderful places to visit, even the awful virtual war zones and other theatres of human tragedy. There too you can triumph, and, on the whole, their rules and laws are dependable and always enforced by the omniscient computer.

But games have the capacity to go much further. Indeed, there are designers who want to use the medium not only to create an environment in which the player is able to triumph, but also to model a better, fairer society for everyone. Video games are exceptional machines for favouring the individual (they do, after all, exist to serve the player, revolving around their every move, responding to their every whim). But they have the capacity to model ways of living that favour everyone, not only the powerful individual. In fact, some of the most popular video games on earth today were designed to do just this.

Richard Bartle grew up in the 1960s on a council estate in Hornsea, Yorkshire. His father was a gas fitter and his mother a school cook at a time in Britain when a person's class defined their expectations. The Bartles, in short, were a working-class family with working-class prospects. After his mother wrote some short children's stories she sent them to a book publisher. The stories were published, scene for scene, but attributed not to his mother but to a well-known children's author at the time. She was given no credit or remuneration. Mrs Bartle no doubt felt the sting of injustice (she kept her original manuscripts and showed them to her son) but she was also resigned to the fact that she was a school cook and that this was to be her place in life. There was no moving up or on.

Stories and games were prevalent in the Bartle household – in addition to his mother's literary ambition, his father was an avid player of board games.

'I invented role-playing games when I was about twelve,' Bartle, who is now fifty-four, tells me. 'I'd stick pieces of paper together and draw a huge map on them. I'd design the world with lakes and mountains. I put various native tribes in the world and I invented a character who had to get from one side of the map to the other.'

Bartle named the game after this lead character, Dr Toddystone. The name was a play on the Victorian explorer Dr Livingstone and the word 'Toddy', British slang in the early 1970s for dog shit.

'I thought the game was going to be dog shit so I named it that,' he says. 'It was an RPG by any measure. I built a diary up of the events that happened in the game: Toddystone having to barter for a horse, being caught in an eclipse and so on. It was . . . vivid.' When he was sixteen Bartle saw his first computer.

'BP opened a chemical works nearby and, as a way to improve relations with the local community, they donated access to their computers to nearby schools,' he says. Bartle's school was allowed to use a DEC System 10 mainframe. He immediately knew that he wanted to use the machine to write a game, but the process was slow. At that time would-be programmers would write their code out by hand. This would then be sent off to an administrator who would type it into the computer. The turnaround for this process was two weeks.

'If you sent something with a bug in it you wouldn't know for a fortnight.'

Bartle's first game featured battling tanks, which could be moved around the map by entering coordinates into the computer. The DEC-10 would then print out a map, using dots to denote the landscape and bracket symbols to show the tank's whereabouts.

'We weren't aware of *Space War* or any of the other games that had been written around the world at that point,' he says. 'But likewise it never occurred to us that people hadn't really written computer games before. We didn't know what they were but we just assumed they were out there.'

For Bartle, his goal in life was simple: find a way to get to university.

'Nobody in my family had ever gone before so it would have made my parents proud,' he says. Bartle was accepted at Essex University ('mainly on flair') and studied mathematics in his first year, along with computer science and physics.

'At the end of the first year there were two students who were better than me at maths and no students better than me at computer science so I switched course entirely,' he says. 'I already had a sense of the injustice of the education system but when I arrived at university it became clearer to me: the other students were just as smart as the kids had been in my school. These students had simply been better taught and better prepped for exams.'

Bartle had the chance to recast these unjust systems when, in his first year of study, he met Nigel Roberts, president of the university's computer society. Roberts then introduced Bartle to Roy Trubshaw, a student in the year above Bartle who, earlier that week, had written the first proof-of-concept for *MUD*, a primitive online adventure game.

'He called it Multi User Dungeon because he wanted to give people a sense of what kind of game it was going to be. Nowadays we call them "Adventure" games, but he also thought "Dungeon" would become the genre's name.' With his prototype, Trubshaw had discovered a way to design a game on the DEC that was shared between multiple users. The pair, assisted by Roberts, expanded the prototype. The total amount of memory available was, at the weekends, just 70k – less than the file size of a photograph taken on a mobile phone today.

By Christmas 1978, *MUD* was playable. Players would sit at a teletype (a device similar to a typewriter that accessed the computer mainframe) and type in commands. There was no screen; details about the world and everyone's actions within it were instead printed out on paper. By the following year the machine code had become 'too unwieldy' to add new things.

'We threw it away and rewrote everything,' says Bartle. 'Most of the game was complete by spring 1980, but Roy's finals were coming so he passed code ownership to me. Roy was mainly interested in programming, with a mild interest in game design. I was the reverse: a slower programmer but sharper with design, so we complemented one another. I added experience points and the idea that a player's character could "level up" and improve their attributes through accomplishments and so on.'

Originally the pair had wanted goals in the game to derive from players themselves. 'But when you're working on something with less computational power than a washing machine, you can't really do that,' he says. 'We had to author gameplay, when originally we had hoped it would be totally emergent.'

By this point, Bartle had become clear in his broader vision for the game.

'We thought the real world sucked,' he says, with the righteous anger of the lifelong revolutionary. 'The only reason I had been allowed into a university is because the country decided that it was so in need of programmers that it was prepared to tolerate people from backgrounds like mine and Roy's in further education. We both railed against that. We wanted to make a world that was better than that. It was a political endeavour right from the start, as well as an artistic one.'

Those political aims manifested in the game through the use of levels and character classes, affording players the freedoms that hadn't been afforded to Bartle, or, at least, to his parents.

'We wanted the game to be pure freedom, to allow people to be themselves,' he says. 'We introduced character classes and levels because I wanted people to have some indication of their own personal merit, based on what they did, rather than where they were born. It's why I'm not a fan of free-to-play games in which you can simply buy progress. That's a complete contravention of what we were trying to do with *MUD*. We were creating a true meritocracy. Not because I thought a meritocracy was the one true way, but if we were going to have a system in which people ranked themselves, then a meritocracy was the least worst approach.'

Bartle excelled in his studies, graduating from Essex with the highest first ever recorded at the time and, as a result, was given the university's solitary PhD grant. *MUD* spread quickly.

'Due to an accident of geography, Essex University was near to a BT research centre at *Martlesham Heath,*' he explains. 'We had access to Experimental Packet Switching Service, through which we could connect to the university of Kent. Through that we could connect to ARPA, the forerunner to the internet. In this way, we could play *MUD* with, say, people from the Massachusetts Institute of Technology. In fact, the head of the MIT media lab was one of the first people to play.'

Students at universities around the country and the world began to create their own versions of *MUD*, each with their own idiosyncrasies and stories.

'There were around twenty different games by 1989,' says Bartle. The most influential was *AberMUD*, named after its birthplace, the University of Aberystwyth, created by Alan Cox, who went on to become one of the co-developers of the Linux operating system.

While, during the 1980s, most of the *MUD* games were similar, in 1989 they began to diverge with the release of *TinyMUD*, a version which stripped out all of the gameplay and was instead a virtual world oriented entirely around socialising.

'You could move around and explore,' says Bartle. 'People went in there and built things, had virtual sex and so on.' Another group of developers reacted against this and started making *MUDs* that emphasised questing over socialising. 'This made a kind of schism between social virtual worlds, and very game-focused games,' says Bartle. 'Both of these branches became distinct. It's the same difference in approach that you see between Alice in Wonderland and Dorothy in Oz. Alice explores and socialises; Dorothy tries to get home.'

The swift propagation of *MUD* was, in part, thanks to Bartle and Trubshaw's decision to give the game away for free to anyone who wanted to play. The pair did this not as a way to get famous or, obviously, to get rich. Rather, in this virtual world, Bartle saw a better blueprint for society. *MUD* was a world in which players were able to progress according to their actions and intelligence rather than through an accident of birth into a certain social class or fortune.

'We wanted the things that were in *MUD* to be reflected in the real world,' he says. 'I wanted to change the world. And, to a certain degree, it worked. There is obviously a difference in style, but nevertheless, in the same way that the latest 3D movie today is fundamentally the same thing as a Charlie Chaplin short, so today's MMOs are *MUD*s,' he says. 'And *MUD* and every subsequent MMO that has adopted its designs are a political statement. I should know: I designed it that way. And if you want the world to change, then making people pay to read your message isn't going to work. So we gave it away.'

Bartle continues to work at Essex University, offering consultancy on some MMO projects in his spare time. Trubshaw left the video-game industry to design systems for air-traffic controllers. Neither man became rich through their game and Bartle believes that he's even less known in his home nation than in America (where, in 2005, he was awarded with the Pioneer prize at the Game Developers Choice Awards).

'Had I been the kind of person who was doing it for monetary gain I wouldn't have been the person to give the code away,' he says. 'Sure, it would be nice if someone who had made a few millions from our ideas came along to give Roy and I some of their winnings. But, when it comes to changing the world, I think we have been successful, to a certain degree. We've shown that virtual worlds can affect the real world. There is progress.'

But that progress is, for Bartle, sluggish.

'I am frustrated at its slow pace,' he says. 'There's so much you can do with virtual worlds. But it's not being done. I wanted them to be places of wonder in which people could go to truly be themselves, away from societal pressure or judgement. My idea was that if you could truly find yourself in a virtual world you might be able to then take that back into the real world. Then we could get rid of these artificial restraints of class, gender, social status and so on that dictate that you are what you are born to be.'

It is a motivating grievance that Bartle, despite his own success, is yet to discard. He still believes in *MUD*'s utopian vision of freedom from inequality and circumstance. The MMO, as it currently stands, may not represent the full blooming of his original seed. But he remains hopeful that these virtual worlds can offer a new way for reality to follow.

'I haven't given up,' he says. 'I want to see the world change before I die.'

Even if players don't recognise it (nor, perhaps, the games' designers) many of the video games we play today have been built in a way that not only reflects the world and its systems, but also attempts to improve its balance. Video games may have morally neutral or ambiguous storylines and they may distract humans away from true progress through the illusion of accomplishment, but at least they provide a place in which everyone who is able to view a screen and make inputs on a controller has a chance to triumph.

Some games, including, arguably, *Call of Duty*, tip into pandering. Triumph is assured. They are rigged in the player's favour in such a way as to make a mockery of success. Other games require their players to work harder in order to prevail (everything from *Dark Souls* to the fan-made hacks of *Super Mario World*, which make the game accessible only to the spatial savant). But in these cases, they mostly play fair, and offer a clear route to triumph for the talented or hard working. This is not guaranteed in life, where success is often the result of an unreplicable recipe involving privilege, education, talent, toil, circumstance and timing. Your chances of falling terminally ill, or starving to death, or becoming CEO of a multinational corporation, are often dictated as much by your circumstances of birth as by your own work and qualities.

Is this fairness what drives people into video games and keeps them there, even to the limits of their well-being? Perhaps not. As we have seen, for some it will be the thrill of competition, for others the chance to discover new places, for others still the social element that surrounds games. Some come for the escapism, a retreat from the troubles of this world, or a place in which to better understand themselves or the systems in which they live. Many come simply because that's where their friends are to be found.

In the early 1990s Richard Bartle came up with a test to sort different kinds of players. The test has its roots in a discussion the game's moderators had over why they played the game: what was it that they got from the experience, and what drew them back?

'This question began a two-hundred-long e-mail chain over a period of six months,' Bartle says. 'Eventually I went through everybody's answers and categorised them. I discovered there were four types of player. I published some short versions of them then, when the journal of *MUD* research came out, I wrote it up as a paper.'

The so-called Bartle test classifies players as Achievers, Explorers, Socialisers or Killers (or a mixture thereof) according to their play-style. Bartle believes that you need a healthy mix of all dominant types in order to maintain a successful MMO ecosystem. Bartle even visits MMO creators today in order to explain his theory to them, and advise them on how to better structure their games to accommodate all types.

'If you have a game full of Achievers (players for whom advancement through a game is the primary goal) the people who arrive at the bottom level won't continue to play because everyone is better than them,' he explains. 'This removes the bottom tier and, over time, all of the bottom tiers leave through irritation. But if you have Socialisers in the mix they don't care about levelling up and all of that. So the lowest Achievers can look down on the Socialisers and the Socialisers don't care. If you're just making the game for Achievers it will corrode from the bottom. All MMOs have this insulating layer, even if the developers don't understand why it's there.'

We've identified, if not different *types* of players, then certainly some of the different ways in which video games appeal to different people. Ultimately, this is what makes video games so fascinating: they are a mirror in which we can discover more about ourselves and individuals and collectives. Either in the way games are designed, or in the way we choose to play them, we can understand more about our urges, and the function that art and entertainment might have in our life.

This is true, perhaps, of all video games, but especially of those which afford us particularly broad freedoms to express ourselves, and especially those which model their world on our own cities and societies.

For that reason, let us return, finally, to Los Santos, the virtual city that is able to accommodate the interests of the Bigfoot hunter, the bedazzled sightseer, the sportsman and the flippantly murderous. A utopia, in its own strange way.

Wait long enough down by the tracks west of the Palomino Highlands at a spot somewhere on Los Santos's left thigh, and eventually a freight train will clacket along. Some of its carriages are insurmountably tall, but others sit empty and ride low enough that, with a spirited jump, you can haul yourself up for a free trip. You won't have the leathery comfort of a stolen German car, or the sky-rollicking freedom of a light aircraft, but there's no better way to see the city. You'll duck under the roaring flyovers of East Los Santos, race the freeway around the Tataviam Mountains, before wheezing through the Grand Senora Desert, where the air has an arid clarity. As you loop around hick town Grapeseed you can gaze over Procopio beach to admire the Pacific as it sets sail into the horizon. Time it right and the sky will start its 5 p.m. bruise into dusk just as you circle back into the city, where the traffic twinkles and skyscrapers stretch with competitive ambition.

You can't talk about *Grand Theft Auto V* without talking about the city. Los Santos exceeds the game in which it's set. *Grand Theft Auto V* is merely something that passes through the city, one of many stories that you pick up every now and again, in between following your own sojourns and distractions.

The idea that cities have personalities is true, but only to a point. They might have an aesthetic, a combination of the man-made and the natural, and their inhabitants might have a peculiar temperament (influenced by the dominant weather or the dominant industry), but in truth, we project our own hopes and insecurities onto the cities we visit or those in which we settle. In them we find what we need to in the moment. This is true of Los Santos, an eager tribute to Los Angeles that blends the real and imagined, and a city that allows you to take from it what you want. It can be a place of both peril and sin as you hold up petrol stations in Davis (the city's gang-torn analogue to Compton). Or it can be a place of peace and leisure as you chase a wild deer through the thin mountain air on a bike.

Here, you can be who you need to be. Want to dress in a tailor-made suit and promenade along the Del Perro pier, with its groan and slop, or swim with sharks in Paleto Bay? Sure thing. Want to listen disapprovingly outside a teenager's bedroom door as he watches porn? Why not? You can live the high life using the proceeds of your stock-market investments, or become a property tycoon. Or you can slum it with the poor: the Harmony town hicks, with their dusty dungarees and moonshine-rosy cheeks, or the shufflers in the projects with their frayed jeans and crack-white eyes. Los Santos, like its analogue Los Angeles, is a city of invention and reinvention: give and take what you need.

This is also true of *Grand Theft Auto V* in general, a game of such scope that it allows us to see what we need to see. You can look at Rockstar's opus as a technological miracle, a game that recreates one of our species's great cities in sound and light, a cathedral of pixels. Or you can look at it as a holiday destination, a place to tumble about with friends, racing mountain bikes or planning heists online. Or a sandbox in which to explore your darker fantasies – cop-killing, hooker-beating, drug-running – all within a consequence-free safe place.

You can see the game's missions as spectacular set pieces. In one you tear down the frontage of a penthouse using a tow truck. In another you attempt to reclaim your yacht and kidnapped son from thieves in a highway chase. Or you can see these moments as failures of impersonation, which recreate the spectacle of television greats such as *The Sopranos* or *The Wire*, but fail to transpose their substance and meaningful human drama. Rockstar undeniably has a talent for mimicry and exaggeration. When it's applied to nature (the waves, the birds, the sun) or to construction (the traffic, the stores, the subway) their work is utterly unrivalled. When it's applied to the movies and TV shows, the results are somewhat charmless. At least, if that's what you choose to see.

You can look at the game as knowing satire. It often successfully skewers Western culture's enormities and failings (even if the satire often has a certain Bansky-esque plainness to it: 'Keep calm and carry on sharing', suggests a poster in the offices of Lifeinvader, Los Santos's version of Facebook). Nevertheless, it's a game that elegantly presents the perils of capitalism: once you've made your money, all that's left to do is learn how to play tennis, race jet-skis or buy up more property. Your purpose is gone. Or maybe you don't buy the satire, and see only weak jokes that throw punches in all directions, and land only few.

You can see the game as anti- (or at least ambivalent towards) women, who appear almost exclusively as objects of desire or ridicule or scorn. Then again, have you met the men? Monsters, the lot of them. If the women dismay in *Grand Theft Auto V* by their absence, the men dismay by their presence. Nobody is likeable here in the city, fuelled by ambition, or grown lazy and aimless with success and wealth. But is their monstrosity and moral repugnancy a problem? To contemporise Henry de Montherlant's phrase that 'happiness writes in white ink on a white page', goodness displays transparent on the screen. Its trio of protagonists, Trevor, Michael and Franklin, are memorable precisely because of their darkness. And perhaps the fact that their (and by association our) heroism is achieved through violence is a cultural failing, rather than that of the writers. The American idea of heroism is, after all, almost always allied with violence.

Grand Theft Auto V, like so many video games, defies straightforward definition or critique because it is simultaneously so many things all at once. As with all cities, when we enter Los Santos we bring with us our own perspectives, hang-ups, ambitions and fears. We embrace or reject them accordingly. Los Santos is a mirror to Los Angeles, but also to the individual. This kind of projection happens with all art and entertainment, but perhaps more so with video games, the only form in which we act. And perhaps more so still in open-world games, in which our freedoms are so broad and so accommodated. And perhaps yet more so still with Los Santos, city of reinvention, through which you can ride a train, and see whatever it is that you need to see.

There's an old saying: 'Wherever you go, there you will be.'

I read it as an amiable warning: it's no use trying to flee yourself. Even if you escape your problems, *you* will always be there. Video games like *Grand Theft Auto V* prove the point, to a certain degree. Unless you're deliberately playing against type, or assuming a specific role, you can't help but bring yourself into the fiction. Your interests and predilections will be reflected in your activity, be it hunting wild animals, racing jet-skis, hiring prostitutes, buying property, planning heists or hiking first thing in the morning. If you are feeling hateful in the real world, the game provides a space in which to act hatefully. Wherever you go, there you will be.

Of course, the way a game is designed will encourage certain types of behaviour, and many interactions that you might wish to make if you were to fully and bodily enter the fiction are entirely closed off. You may only be able to interact with the world around you via a gun's sights. There is no option in many video games to eat, to love, to touch, to comfort or any of the other crucial verbs with which we live life. Nevertheless, the medium's greatest draw is surely the way in which it allows us to understand more about ourselves and the world, in a safe place, through the mystical act of play. Video games may be escapism, but wherever you escape to, there too you will be, and there you might just find yourself.

Back in Tainan City, in an internet café popular with players close to the one in which Chen Rong-Yu died, there's an attitude among players that death by gaming is something that happens to other people, people with bigger problems and deeper issues.

'I've never played for longer than forty-eight hours at a time,' says twenty-two-year-old Ding Kuo Chih, who has been playing games in internet cafés for a decade. 'Nowadays I rarely play for longer than ten hours at a stretch. I heard about the guy who died. My friends and I were just talking about it, actually. We all think it's just ridiculous to play a game to death. The guy must have had some financial problems or something. Perhaps that's what happened – he chose to spend all his money on video games, so he had no money to eat and drink properly. Something like that.'

Every player in the café has heard of the 'death by video game' stories, but they appear to have had little impact on behaviour.

'It's not really changed anything for me,' says Chiu, a mousy girl who's playing *Starcraft*. 'Maybe he had some problem with his heart? It wouldn't happen to me. I have a job.'

Likewise, for sixteen-year-old Shih, Rong Yu's death seems irrelevant.

'It's not changed anything for me,' he says. 'I am an infrequent gamer. I only come here once a week, so it's OK for me to play for a long stretch of time. I am just killing time.'

And what better place to kill time? Video games, at times, bring comfort. Often they bring challenge, relief, glory, discovery, even a glimpse of a fairer existence. They reward you for your efforts with empirical, unflinching fairness. Work hard in a game and you advance. Take the path that's opened to you and persevere with it and you can save the world. Every player is given an equal chance to succeed. There is a prelapsarian quality to video games that makes them irresistible, especially to people whose experiences in life have been of injustice and unfairness.

Video games are truly a metaphor for a vision of life that can be ordered, understood and conquered. They may start off as broken places, full of conflict and violence, but they are utopias too, in that the things that are broken can be put right. Hour by hour, in most video games, our work is to restore, rescue and perfect these virtual worlds.

But, as the experiences of Rong Yu and all of the others demonstrate, this is not the entire story. Video games can also distract, depress, have a negative impact on health. They can enforce problematic values in profound ways and even lead people away from more effective and important support systems in their lives. Yes, video games can be a useful tool in finding refuge, but they could never replace family or friendships, the natural and fundamental supports of human beings.

Video games can inspire greatness and challenge the status quo, pointing out flaws in our systems, illustrating better ways of living and ruling. In this way they can shape our attitudes, beliefs and values, perhaps in a more immediate, physical way than other media. But of course, this same power can be used in damaging ways. Video games also have the capacity to demoralise people, and vividly reinforce systems of power, privilege and even oppression.

No, video games won't save you – they might even kill you – and the jury is still very much out as to whether they improve or imperil the world.

But the potential – that shimmering, vivid, endlessly exciting potential – is there, fizzing on the restless screen. Therefore, so too are we.

Killing time.

Acknowledgements

Special thanks to each of the editors with whom I have worked and from whom I have inevitably learned so much.

In particular: Nicholas Thompson, Matt Buchanan, Jay Caspian Kang, Alan Burdick and Anthony Lydgate of the *New Yorker*. Bobby Baird of *Harper's* magazine. Keith Stuart of the *Guardian*. Tony Mott, Joao Sanchez, Margaret Robertson and Alex Wiltshire of *Edge*. Tom Bramwell, Oli Welsh, Ellie Gibson and Martin Robinson of *Eurogamer*, Stephen Totilo of Kotaku, Chris Suellentrop of the *New York Times* and Matter, Kris Graft and Simon Carless of Gamasutra, Will Knight of *MIT Technology Review*, Greg J. Smith of HOLO and Helen Lewis of the *New Statesman*.

Thanks to Tom Bissell, for reading the manuscript before anyone else, for giving me an example to follow and the encouragement and belief to keep going.

Thank you, Christian Donlan, Brian Taylor, Kieron Gillen, Robert Howells, Will Porter, Ste Curran, Ann Scantlebury, Ed Hawkins and Tom Fenwick for your friendship, camaraderie and advice. To Owain Bennallack for 'chronoslip' and for your shrewdness and encouragement.

To Steven Poole for showing us all how it should be done with such grace and elegance through the years.

To Jane Finigan, for her ever-present support and guidance, and to the team at Serpent's Tail, who have worked so hard to make and chaperone this book. In particular, thank you to Nick Sheerin and Michael Bhaskar.

Thank you to my brother, with whom I first shared a joystick, to my grandmother, who bought me my first Game Boy, to my mother for her care and to my father for his lyricism. To my wife, who can still lose a day with *Animal Crossing*, and to my children, who each week reveal new reasons to appreciate the unique power of video games, and new reasons to be wary.

Index